Complicity and Conviction

William Hubbard

Complicity and Conviction:
Steps toward an Architecture of Convention

The MIT Press
Cambridge, Massachusetts, and London, England

Second printing, January 1981
© 1980 by
The Massachusetts Institute of Technology

This book was set in VIP Optima by
Village Typographers, printed by Halliday
Lithograph, and bound by The Alpine Press
Inc., in the United States of America.

Opposite: Sketch by Le Corbusier of a
jardin suspendu

Library of Congress Cataloging in
Publication Data

Hubbard, William.
  Complicity and conviction.

  Bibliography: p.
  Includes index.
  1. Architecture—Psychological aspects.
2. Architecture—Philosophy. I. Title.
NA2540.H82   720'.1   80—16240
ISBN 0—262—08106—7

A
500
182
980

Contents

Contents

Preface

Anyone who sets out to write a book soon finds that simple inner motivation is never quite equal to the task, but must be supplemented by the time and support and encouragement and guidance that can come only from others. In my case, time was provided by an open-ended leave of absence from my architectural firm, Glave Newman Anderson & Associates, of Richmond, Virginia. The studies that filled that time would have been impossible without the generous financial support of the Ernest A. Grunsfeld Memorial Fund of Chicago. And at two crucial points in this work, I might well have pitched over the whole project had it not been for the confidence and faith (completely unwarranted at that early stage) shown to me by two friends, Bruce Bonacker and Kay Riley. But none of this would have led to a concrete result without the encouragement and guidance so freely given me over the past five years by Stanford Anderson of MIT. From him I received a sustaining vision of what architecture can be.

That vision begins from the realization that in the course of living out our daily lives we unwittingly enact patterned regularities of which we are not fully conscious. Much of our living in buildings is done in this unconsciously patterned way, and the shape of our buildings is, to a certain extent, a reflection, even a record, of such unintended patterns. But a building, we all know, is more than an artifact; it is also a conscious creation. And because it is we who do that creating, it is within our power to decide which patterns a building will reflect. Not only can we shape a building to accommodate the activities that we intend to carry on there; we can also give that building a form that will either support or inhibit patterns that we will bring into existence unintentionally. We can consciously shape a building to manipulate what we will later do there unconsciously.

But in order to use buildings in this way we must open up our attitudes about unconsciously enacted patterns. We must avoid both the putatively humanistic attitude that confers esteem upon any pattern that results from human action, as well as the seemingly scientific attitude that denies the worth of any pattern that is other than the one consciously intended by the actor. For when we make such blanket judgments beforehand, we abdicate our freedom by surrendering our capacity to make decisions to a standard outside the direct control of our will. What we want is the ability to stand as free critics of our own actions, to judge our own actions on the basis of our reaction to the consequences those actions are likely to produce. To do that, we need to know the unseen connections between what we do and what eventually happens. To disclose those unseen connections is, I think, the proper role of analysis. Analysis ought to arm us with that knowledge so that we can decide which of our actions we want to keep up, which we want to stop, even which ones we might want to adopt from other circumstances. But what standard of judgment can we use to make such decisions? Quite apart from finding a standard we can agree upon, what standard of judgment could avoid that surrender of volition of the other, "beforehand" standards?

Stan Anderson supplied me with an answer, at once simple and profound, in the question, "Does it expand human possibility?" We can look at the ways we act, we can look at each of the ways we build, and ask ourselves: Does building in that manner bring about a situation in which we have more ways to have genuine effect in the world? Or does building in that manner leave us with fewer ways, or with ways that have only trivial effects?

In an ideal world we would all ask such questions of our buildings, but in actuality that will not happen. The questions will be asked only if someone asks them for us. The job of asking those questions falls, I think, to the architectural critic. And it is a role that is both real and necessary, for to answer those questions is to point out to us the ways of building that free us for effective action in the world. And to do that is to provide people with at least a portion of the means by which they can take control of the quality of their own lives. That is the kind of criticism I have tried to do here.

Complicity and Conviction

Talking about an Architecture of Convention

Let me draw a radical distinction. Let me say that there are two ways in which reality makes sense to us: there are those things we accept as being the way they are because we have no choice but to do so, and there are those things we accept as being the way they are because we want them to be that way. That is, with the first the arrangement could not have been otherwise and so we accede to that fact; with the second the arrangement could have been otherwise, but we prefer that it be this way instead.

For the time of this book, let us call the first category of things inevitable and the second, conventional. Inevitable things include such concrete arrangements as the shape of trees and mountains and of people themselves; and they also include such intangible things as laws of nature, forces operative in the world like gravity or natural selection.

Conventional things can likewise be concrete or intangible. Human ethics, the ways we act toward each other, are intangible conventional arrangements. We could choose to act toward each other in any number of ways, but from that number there are certain ways of acting that we prefer. Conventional arrangements can also be concrete, as in the clothes we wear (the way we prefer to look) or in the way we depict those trees and mountains (the way we prefer them to look). Even the fact that we depict those trees on flat rectangles of canvas—that, too, is conventional. We do it because doing so feels right to us.

These conventions of art especially concern us here, for in the creative act the matter of how we prefer things to be is brought to sharpest focus. More than in most fields of endeavor, an artist can, almost literally, make his work be anything. Every artist knows this, and at each moment he must ask, "How will I decide what to do and what not to do?" The question is at the crux of every creative act. It is a question that people who do not create are often not fully aware of. Writers talk of the terror of confronting a blank page, artists know the terror of a blank canvas. And even though patronage, the marketplace, and the concerns of the moment can all influence what is put upon that blankness, none of those factors ever provides a full answer to the question, How will I decide what to do and what not to do?

One approach has always been to rely upon one's feelings, to arrange and rearrange forms on that blankness until the configuration feels right. Artists have created in this way for centuries; the methods they have used to juggle those forms have sometimes been codified, sometimes stated only vaguely or even left implicit; but always the test, at the end of the juggling, "Does it feel right to my sensibility, to my taste?" At base, the artist accepted his own sensibility as the standard against which to judge what to do, a sensibility that could have been otherwise.

If there is one characteristic that links the diverse art movements of the modernist period, it is perhaps a hyperawareness of the fact that one's personal sensibility could have been otherwise. A modernist artist is so deeply aware of this possibility of otherwise-ness that he feels a deep unease about simply accepting his own sensibility. He feels a need for some reason that will convince him that he ought to feel one way and not another. And so he searches for such a reason. He tries to open himself to conditions that are not conventional but inevitable, to conditions that exist apart from him and his arbitrary likes and dislikes, to forces at work in the world that produce inevitable effects, effects therefore undistorted by arbitrary preferences. His goal becomes to attain a sensibility such that he will prefer what he finds when he thus opens himself, that his sensibility will replicate the action of those forces at work, that he will become as a conduit for those forces to "work their will."

This search for forces at work has led in many directions. We can see a succession of such forces in the history of modern art: encountered visual reality, the physiological effects of color, the unfettered fantasies of the subconscious mind, the automatic movements of the hand, the unselfconscious production of the marketplace, the nature of paint, or the nature of the flat surface itself.

One can see the same motivation to flee the conventional at work in modern architecture; only in architecture we settled early upon function as the untainted, inevitable force at work. One should (the doctrine went) be open to the forms produced when function determines the shape of things. The architect should replicate the effect of those forces. He should discover the form that would have resulted had those functional requirements been able to determine their own form. Thus the fascination during the twenties with grain elevators, cars, airplanes—all (ostensibly) untainted by arbitrary sensibility, all the direct products of the force at work of functional requirements.

And indeed it is largely because of the modernist doctrine that we have all "opened ourselves" and now do feel within ourselves an appeal that comes from knowing what an object does and sensing how appropriate the form is to that function (the appeal of a suspension bridge or of Shaker furniture). But there is another kind of appeal in which something feels right even though we don't know or don't consider what it does (a fabric design, for example). That second appeal is the appeal of a conventional arrangement. By the force of its form upon our expectations, without verbal rationalization of why we ought to like it, it persuades us to want it to be the way it is.

The point I want to argue for is that both architects and viewers, in their attention to the first kind of appeal, have lost sight of the second, to the extent that society now sees conventional appeal as not the province of architecture, not one of the things that architecture provides. Furthermore, the concept is a self-fulfilling one. Architects don't provide conventional appeal in new buildings, so people don't encounter it; never seeing it in buildings, people don't expect it; not expecting it, they don't ask architects to provide it. "Modern buildings just don't appeal to me the way old buildings do," goes the refrain. People arrive quite naturally at the idea that architecture can do no more for us than it does, because hardly anybody has seen a modern building that does do more.

But it isn't just modernist buildings that lack this kind of appeal. The architecture that is seen as the alternative to modernism also fails to provide it. The work of Venturi, Graves, Eisenman, Meier—none of it really "comes to us" in the way premodern buildings do. It doesn't persuade us to "want the shapes to be the way they are." But not just that—it fails even to forestall us from wondering "why this thing is the shape it is." Looking at postmodern buildings, we become so aware of how easily the arrangement could have been otherwise that we feel imposed upon; the arrangement feels capricious and we are dissatisfied.

We can see why postmodern buildings leave us with this feeling. The best modernist buildings have at least the appeal of a quasi-inevitability—the shapes seem justified by the requirements. But when the postmoderns rejected the idea that an arrangement of forms could be inevitable, they failed to come up with an alternative way of convincing us to accept the arrangements they do give us. They threw out one kind of appeal without picking up on the other.

There was good reason for rejecting the modernist doctrine that an architecture could be made to flow, conduit-like, from a body of facts. Critics like Stanford Anderson have pointed to the arrogance and coerciveness of such a position, its implication that if you do not like such an architecture, then the fault is not in the architecture but in you. If you do not accede to the "revealed truth" in these forms that are as inevitable as the rocks and trees, then you are being retardataire, sentimental, irrational. In thus clearing the air of unexamined cant, the critique by the postmoderns has been both salutary and necessary. Despite that, they still do not see architecture as something that has to convince people to want it. Again, when they threw out the appeal of inevitability, they did not pick up on the appeal of conventionality. It is as if they did not recognize any need for a building to appeal, to convince.

But it was perhaps only natural that they would think this way. There are two camps of postmodernism and both have reached the conclusion that buildings need not appeal, but each came to it by a different route. The two attitudes are normally labeled elitist and populist, but that oversimplifies the situation. The first attitude might better be characterized as "there are things that matter more than what people like," while the second carries the implication that "nothing matters more than what people like."

(In practice, of course, no architect of talent fits neatly into boxes like these. His works are always greater than any box we could construct, and when we do push his works into such a box, important parts get sliced off. But there are aspects of the first tendency in the work of Eisenman, Graves, and Meier, while the second attitude appears in the work of Venturi.)

The first group would reject the idea that a design can be proved to be inevitable— that an objective test, one that doesn't involve our opinions, could show one design to be the only correct solution. But they would hold onto the parallel idea that there are objective standards that exist apart from us. They would hold to an ideal of quality, the view that a designer's primary obligation is to provide his design with an inner integrity, a design consistency. There is no call for selling that kind of consistency to an audience, persuading them to want the design to be consistent in this way and not in some other way. Of course, having an audience prefer the design is always desirable, but it is not of primary importance since the public is not the final arbiter of a building's worth. The true worth of a building is determined by how much integrity it has, how well it meets those objective standards of quality. To someone holding to such a view of design, the idea of taking pains to persuade people to "want it to be this way" would be like working to convince someone to prefer "to be or not to be" over "whether to be or not." To such a person, the quality, the superiority, of the first would be so beyond question that to sell it would be to cheapen it. For when I try to sell you on something (that is, truly engage you as an equal and not just patronize you), I implicitly admit that there might be something just as good that a reasonable person like yourself might choose—a choice from which I want to dissuade you. If I believed a design to be good beyond question, then not only would I see no need to convince an audience of its worth, I would want to avoid the whole activity of selling.

Under the second postmodernist tendency there would be no call for selling a design to an audience, but in this case that conclusion is reached by a different route. This second tendency would hold that public opinion *is* the final arbiter of a building's worth, that a design ought to provide what the viewers will be expecting, and that if there is any standard of quality at all, it is that the best designs are the ones that most precisely and completely meet those expectations. The goal, then, is to produce a design that will meet with such immediate acceptance that any explaining or persuading would be superfluous. Indeed, if any viewer were to need explaining or persuading before accepting the design, that would indicate that the design had failed to meet its goal of matching the viewer's expectations. The fault would be in the building, not the viewer.

This second postmodern tendency thus reverses the modernist implication that the fault for an unappreciated design lies with the viewer and not with the building. But in that curious way that philosophical positions so often do, this tendency returns full circle to the more basic modernist tenet, the idea that the designer ought to become as a conduit for forces at work in the world, neither distorting nor influencing the free flow those forces would have had if the designer had not been there. To give an audience all and only what they expect is to treat those expectations as if they were such forces at work.

But more to the point, it is an attempt "not to be there": to give an audience only what it already expects is to avoid engaging that audience. Curiously then, under neither postmodern tendency—neither this populist one nor the first, elitist, one—does the designer engage his audience.

In contrast, the whole point of what I will be calling an architecture of convention would be for the designer to actively engage people's perceptions and expectations, to manipulate them and be shaped by them. I talked at the beginning about the appeal of conventional things. The modernists rejected such appeal, and the postmoderns misunderstand it. But earlier ages saw such conventional things as the privileged province of the artist. It is this province that I want to reclaim for architecture. But to do that requires that the architect learn once again how to engage his audience. He must learn how to create a configuration of forms that has such appeal, that feels so right, that an audience wouldn't want it to be any other way. The architect has to be able to give his audience a way of finding, within those forms, *a reason for wanting those forms to be the way they are* and not any of the other ways they might have been. The skill of such an architect would be his ability to appeal to his audience—sometimes giving them precisely what would feel right to their sensibilities of the moment, but also, in the greatest cases, presenting them with forms strong enough actually to make them recast those sensibilities. The true raw material of such an architect, the stuff he would work and shape, would be the sensibilities and expectations of his audience. He would play with them—play upon them—the way an actor plays with and upon the expectations of his audience. And just as an actor knows, so this architect would know that no matter how perfect the performance, no matter how much it pleased him as a creator, the audience would be the final arbiter. But not the audience as an abstraction, frozen into one state that is beyond reach; rather, the real audience, the flesh-and-blood expectations that a skillful architect could guide by the force of his forms. That audience, the influenced audience, would be the final arbiter of an architecture of convention.

There are methods of accomplishing this high-wire act of influencing an audience while appealing to it, and the purpose of this book is to rediscover them and describe them so that they can again be used. But before I can set out on that course, I feel I must first clear away an idea that would block our path, the idea that there might be an architecture of the past that would so fully do what I say an architecture of convention should do, that we might simply reach back and design that way again. One tempting candidate would be the American architecture of the late nineteenth and early twentieth centuries that we have come to call Scenographic—the work that begins with Richardson and the Shingle Style, encompasses the more picturesque classical works of McKim, Mead & White and John Russell Pope, and ends with the evocative work of Goodhue and the collegiate Gothic work of the twenties. The idea is tempting. Here was an architecture that had undeniable popular appeal but which seldom pandered to the crowd, an architecture that worked upon and with people's expectations. The idea is all the more tempting because we have come to suspect that the Scenographic might have been precipitously jettisoned in the rush to join the modernist bandwagon—that it might thus have potential that we could explore if we could somehow pick up the threads and restart it in our own day.

The idea of restarting a movement that was prematurely abandoned has particular appeal for the way we think just now. The idea manages to tap both our renewed veneration for things old and our new ecological ethic of making the best use of the things we already have. But even in the face of this, I want to contend that the Sceno-graphic, even if it had been allowed to run its course, would never have been able to provide all that an architecture should provide. The Scenographic was an inadequate style. It gave its audience a reason for wanting it to be the way it was, but it was not enough of a reason. In the first chapter I will detail the nature of this inadequacy. I will show why the Scenographic, for all its appeal, could never serve as the proper model for an architecture of convention—that the proper models can be found only by looking elsewhere, even outside the realm of architecture.

The Scenographic Style
as a Model for an Architecture of Convention

Though it may have been insufficient, the Scenographic style did give its audiences a reason for wanting the forms to be that way. It was perhaps the last style that recognized the necessity for providing such a reason, and its designers were perhaps the last group of designers who possessed the skill to do so. For that reason we can learn a great deal from the Scenographic designers—so long as we keep constantly in mind that we have to do *more* than they did.

The primary lesson I want to draw from this look at the Scenographic is a clear conception of what it means to engage an audience. It is quite easy to fall into the trap of thinking that just because an architecture appeals to us it must therefore be engaging us: in actuality, "appealing" forms are often not engaging us at all. There is, for example, the situation in which both the designer and the audience like the forms, but the audience's reason for preferring that the forms be that way has nothing to do with the designer's intentions in causing them to be that way. Such a situation might be, on the one hand, only a coincidence, in which the designer's taste, as it followed its own course of development, just happened to cross the taste of the audience as it developed. Or it might be a situation in which the designer was cynically playing to the values of the audience while holding to another set of values for himself. Clearly both situations are untenable. The first situation collapses with the mere unfolding of time.

As the designer follows his course and we follow ours, we come to realize that our reasons for liking the work had been unfounded, fatuous. The second situation, even more cruel, collapses when we act upon our delight in the work and inquire into its origins. When we learn the designer's true motives, we feel deceived; far from seeing the work as appealing, we now see that it mocks us and our values.

The Scenographic style largely avoided these situations. The thoughts on the minds of the designers were not always the thoughts of the audience, but there was enough similarity, enough correspondence, so that we can fairly say that they were "engaged." The test for this—in fact the test of whether any architecture is really engaging its audience—is to compare the answers to these two questions:

Knowing that he can do virtually anything, on what basis does the designer decide what to do and what not to do?

Knowing that the forms they are presented with could have had any shape (or at least not assuming that they "had to be" any particular shape), on what basis does the audience decide which shape to prefer and which not to prefer?

With the Scenographic style, both groups arrived at a preference by the implicit standard: The shape we prefer is the shape that makes the best picture. This was the common basis upon which the two groups engaged. The audience had a vague, unstructured feeling about how they wanted pictures to look, and they wanted buildings that would "look like that." And designers had a set of standards that systematized those feelings about pictures and made them explicit, and they had techniques by which they could arrive at forms that had the look of "good pictures."

This disparity in explicitness is natural and probably inevitable: a designer needs more than the vague feeling about what he likes that will suffice for a viewer. If a designer truly had nothing more than this vague feeling, then the only way he could work would be to produce all the shapes possible and then pick the one that most appealed to that feeling. No artist really works this way. Each uses some sort of working system to guide him toward a much smaller set of things. He uses that system because he knows that when he works that way he will be more likely to produce things that might appeal to his particular sensibility, and from those things he can pick the ones he likes best.

What do I mean by "shapes that make the best picture"? I can best explain by using the renderings of buildings produced for popular magazines of that era, the pen and pencil renderings reproduced not only in trade publications but in magazines for general readership. To a degree that seems remarkable today, the illustrators of the 1880s and after were able to free themselves from a preoccupation with what the form (physically) was and open themselves to how the form *looked*. Their renderings describe, with remarkable fidelity, the visual effects produced by the forms, and not the forms themselves. More accurately, they are a record of the preferred appearance of each form, that is, not the shape that the form would have at all times and under all light conditions but rather, of all the appearances that form could produce, the one appearance that the renderer preferred.

What kinds of appearances were preferred? Look at Ernest Peixotto's pen sketch of an Italian church (figure 1). Only the shadows and textures of the stucco forms are recorded, the edges that we know are there disappear into the sky. And this dissolving of forms takes place not just with sun-bleached stucco but with walls of stone and brick and with roofs of shingle and slate (figure 2). Eldon Deane, in the mid-eighties, turned the same Impressionist eye on Shingle Style houses and produced vignettes of such economy that they consist virtually of nothing except the visual effects that struck him as dominant in each scene (figure 3).

Obviously few buildings could present just this appearance to a viewer at any given time, but each part of the building, under the right conditions, could present such an appearance. It is *this* appearance that the renderer has chosen for recording, and he has chosen it because it is the appearance that he most preferred. Now, when the people of

Figure 1. Drawing by Ernest Peixotto of the Chiesa dei Miracoli, Brescia, Italy.

Figure 2. Drawing by Bertram Goodhue of a house near Greenwich, Connecticut.

Figure 3. Pencil vignettes by
E. Eldon Deane.

Mr. · Migginson's · House · Pride's Crossing
McKim · Mead & White : Architects.
Sturgis & Brigham :

that era experienced such a building over time, they would come to see all the varied appearances that each of its parts could present; if they shared the renderer's opinion about which appearances were preferable, those preferred appearances would likely be the ones that would stick in their memory. We might say that such a rendering records the way a person experiencing the actual building would have remembered the building. I think it not too implausible even to say that the image of a building recorded by the popular renderers is very like the image that a person of the time would have carried in his head.

So then, what is the character of that image? Look at a stunning example of the era's renderings, a drawing of a church by Bertram Goodhue (figure 4). Look at the roof, how the shadow cast by the main tower is touched with white, both along the standing seams and in the pans. The texture, the visual feel of that roof, is the same in both light and shade. Noticing this, we become aware of the breadth of treatment of this rendering: passages with a similar visual feel flow across large areas of the rendering even as the relative darkness and the tone of those passages change dramatically. Look again at the sweep of the roof, even as it goes from black to white to black. Or look at any of Goodhue's shingle roofs or stone walls (figure 5). The treatment varies across the

Figure 4. Rendering by Goodhue
of a church proposed for
Westminster, Massachusetts.

Figure 5. Rendering by Goodhue
of the cloister of St. Thomas's
College, Washington, D.C.

surface of the form, but always in such a way that the eye moves easily across and over the areas of changing tone but similar texture.

But note that the eye does not just wander about. It is drawn to definite places in the rendering by brilliant tonal contrasts, dark shapes next to light shapes. Look again at Goodhue's Winchester Church, how the pale turret at the right draws the eye by its being set in the nearly black field of the apse roof. Then see how that black roof turns white as it nears the front of the church so that the eye is drawn to the main tower by the large dark shapes of window, roof shadow, and tree set in the nearly white field formed out of the sky and the sun-bleached tower and roof.

In terms we would use today, we would say that the overall rendering has a breadth of treatment that causes the eye to move across the depicted surfaces and that it has a pattern of dark-light contrasts that draws the eye toward selected focal points. If we are at all justified in calling this a "good picture" (and the people of the time most certainly did), then we can say that those qualities are among the ones that made it so. Those qualities, that look, was the look that people wanted their pictures to have. To be thought a good picture, a rendering had to have that look. To be thought a good building, each experienced part of it had to be able to present that look—to somebody, at some time.

How can we know the people of that era really felt that way? Were there spokesmen who actually said that a picture or a building had to have qualities like these in order to be considered good?

The answer is yes, and we can find their statements in the popular drawing hand-books of the era, the books addressed to the amateur who wanted to teach himself how to make good pictures. Luckily for this study, these books predate the notion of drawing as an almost therapeutic means of expressing or revealing the inner self. For these authors, there were no mysteries about drawing, no questions that "only you can answer for yourself." Drawing, for them, was technique. Everything that one might need to know could be spelled out in explicit detail. Two of the most explicit—and (consequently?) influential—handbooks come from opposite ends of the era: John Ruskin's *Elements of Drawing* of 1856 (continually reprinted and excerpted through the turn of the century)[1] and Arthur Guptill's *Rendering in Pen and Ink* of the 1920s (one of a long series of handbooks Guptill produced up through the 1950s).[2] The handbooks of course deal with much more than breadth, contrast, and focus, but let us look at what each author says about these visual effects.

Both writers begin by showing their students how to lay down a tone on the paper. Ruskin advises his reader to draw a series of small squares and fill each with closely spaced parallel lines, making some boxes uniformly dark, some uniformly light. But he cautions readers against extremes of light and dark. A good drawing has ". . . pure white only at the extreme brightest highlights—all else must have a tone."[3] And shadows, he warns, should never be "black nor approaching black, they should be evidently and always of a luminous nature"—an effect achieved by leaving touches of the white paper to show among the black ink lines.[4]

Guptill, almost sixty years later, takes his students through a similar set of exercises: he shows a great variety of graded tones and uniform tones[5] (figure 6) that are shot through with white sparkle. And if luminosity was Ruskin's goal, Guptill too has his reasons for wanting sparkle. A good rendering, he says, should tell the viewer what sort of material is being depicted, and sparkling tones tell how light reflects off the variations in a surface; even stucco should have a few black specks to tell of its roughness. Shadows too should reveal the material on which they fall, by means of touches of light among the darks (figure 7).[6]

Both teachers also counsel their students to give their pictures a strong focus, and they say that this is best done by opposing masses of dark and light at the focal point. Ruskin reminds his readers that "Of course the character of everything is best manifested by Contrast . . . light is exhibited by darkness, darkness by light."[7] We should use

Figure 6. Exercises by Arthur
Guptill for laying down tones
with ink lines.

Figure 7. Sketches by Guptill
depicting texture in shadows.

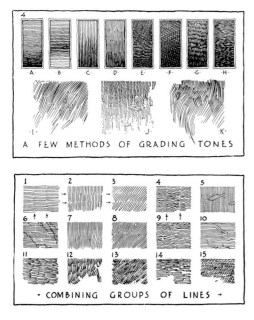

Figure 8. Diagrams and examples by Guptill of focus achieved by tonal contrast.

WHITE AGAINST BLACK·SURROUNDED BY GRAY

BLACK AGAINST WHITE·SURROUNDED BY GRAY

LIGHT CENTER SURROUNDED BY BLACK FADING INTO GRAY

DARK CENTER SURROUNDED BY WHITE · CORNERS GRAY

this fact to give our pictures the quality Ruskin calls "breadth"—"A large gathering of each kind of thing into one place; light being gathered to light, darkness to darkness, colour to colour."[8] But we must be careful how we achieve this focused contrast, "a too manifest use of the artifice vulgarises a picture."[9] We want the contrast to appear as if it occurred naturally; our goal should be to "assemble all the circumstances which will naturally produce white in one place and brown in another."[10]

Guptill makes the same point in a series of diagrams and pictures. He shows how the eye is naturally drawn to the point of greatest contrast, but he also points to the desirability of mitigating the unbroken intensity of the white or black. If the contrasts are mitigated in an artful way, a picture can have dramatic focus and still avoid an artificial, forced look—a point he illustrates with examples (figure 8).[11]

But if contrast is desirable at the focal point, then it must also be a desirable quality for the other areas of the picture. How can one achieve this overall contrast? The answer for both authors is simultaneous variation of tones. Ruskin points to the desirability of "darken[ing] a tree trunk as long as it comes against a light sky, and throw[ing] sunlight on it precisely at the spot where it comes against a dark hill."[12]

Guptill uses a rendering by Goodhue to illustrate the principle (figure 9):

As a splendid example of the use of graded tones for bringing about contrasts where desired, refer to the drawing by Goodhue. Here the left side of the building is shown practically white, surrounded by a gray of clouds and foliage and shadows. Towards the right, the building has been gradually darkened, especially along the roof and chimney, until it counts as a dark tone against a white sky. . . . See how the hedge has been handled, for instance, in such a way that light counts against dark along its entire length.[13]

Thus, the visual character that we apprehend in the renderings is the visual character the artists intended to produce. They were aware of those visual qualities of breadth, contrast, and focus; they valued them; and they had techniques for producing them in pictures.

All of which brings us to our second question. Did the architects of the time decide what to do by asking themselves which forms would best produce these visual effects—which forms would produce the look of a good picture? Again the answer can be found by looking in the handbooks of the era, this time at the technique of *indication*.

Then and now (perhaps always), an architect develops a design through a series of increasingly explicit projective sketches. Each sketch is a drawing in its own right, but

Figure 9. Rendering by Goodhue
of the parish house of St. Peter's
Church, Morristown, New Jersey.

uppermost in the architect's mind are the real building forms that could be projected from the sketch.[14] The sketches at the earliest stages of the evolution leave so much unspecified that each could be projected into a great number of possible buildings, each building true to the sketch. As the sketches develop, however, they become more explicit, and this explicitness decreases the number of possibilities that could faithfully be projected from each. The process of developing a design, then, has the element of gradually closing down options until one solution is reached for every aspect of the building. The architect thus draws his sketch in order to stand in judgment of it. At every stage he has to decide what to take out of the sketch (and thus out of his building), what to change, and what to carry forward into the next stage. One way the architects of the Scenographic era made these decisions was to ask themselves, "What will make this sketch a good picture?"

Look, for example, at a sketch by H. H. Richardson (or a draftsman of his)[15] from an early stage in the development of the design for the Marshall Field Wholesale Store (figure 10). The designer has drawn little more than a pattern of lights and darks, but already the arrangement "makes a good picture." Although those marks were studied as if they were only tones, Richardson knew that they were also indications of real

Figure 10. Early sketch by H. H.
Richardson for the Marshall Field
Wholesale Store.

forms. Because of this, even though all the marks in the sketch may look equivalent, there are really three different kinds of marks. There are the marks that represent known forms: those white dashes left at the spring line of the big arches are certain to become heavy window mullions in a later sketch, and from the eyebrow shapes over the small arches we can be certain that the designer is studying the visual effect of Richardson's characteristic molded arches. But there are other marks that represent no particular element; deciding what they might become can be deferred until a later sketch. Some of these marks would be added "to make a better sketch," but others would be happy accidents—unintentional marks that were kept and carried forward because they made the sketch a better sketch. For example, it is interesting to speculate that the draftsman's practice of ending each line in a blob or tick mark might have been the source for this decoration on the extrados of the arch of the Crane Library (figure 11): the blob appeared at the end of a line in an early sketch, it made the sketch look better, and so was carried forward through the series.

Most often, though, indications were added intentionally, usually in response to the architect's intuitive feel for "what the sketch needed." Sometimes the architect would have a personal system of indications, as with the eyebrow shapes just seen. Sometimes

Figure 11. H. H. Richardson, Crane Library, Quincy, Massachusetts, elevation and detail.

the indications would even be codified, as in the suggestions for capturing the visual effect of the various orders[16] published in David Varon's 1916 *Indication in Architectural Design* (figures 12, 13).

But more interesting are the indications that architects put in their sketches without a definite form in mind. We can see this sort of indication in sketches for buildings in the collegiate Gothic style. Take, for example, the sketch by Charles Z. Klauder shown in figure 14. The drawing is a "good picture," especially in the way it directs the way our eyes move over it. Squint at this drawing and focus on the left face of the tower: the eye starts at the oriel on the ground, moves up the outer corner buttresses, then shifts into the center to rise up to the peak of the topmost arch, where the eye is held, at the point that is both the focus of the drawing and the major feature of the building. We need only our simple lessons from Ruskin and Guptill to see how the sketch does this. From the black oriel set in a white field we move to white piers flanked by the dark trees and the shadows of the lower window. As we ascend, the piers turn gray against the white sky, so the eye follows the white, where it finds the deepest black, set in a white field surrounded by grays. Following the contrast, we rise to the top of the black arch, but are stopped from slipping too easily into the white sky by a gray texture above the head of

Figure 12. David Varon, sketches of ways to indicate the orders, in elevation and in perspective.

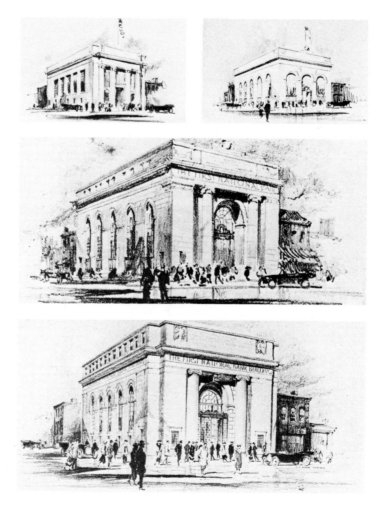

Figure 13. Technique of indication used to develop building facades, showing a design as presented, approved, and built.

Figure 14. Crayon sketch by
Charles Z. Klauder for the tower
at Concordia Seminary, St. Louis.

the opening. Note how indication will carry this image into the actual building: Klauder will make certain that the oriel is given thin mullions to keep it looking black, he will keep the lower parts of those piers smooth and simple, he will keep the embrasure of the lower window deep but simple, and he will elaborate the upper piers—perhaps by multiplying them, perhaps by crockets, anything so long as it casts a lot of shadows. At the top of the arch he will again keep his embrasure clean, but he will do something to darken the opening, perhaps louvers or a black metal screen. Finally, he will elaborate the panel above the arch: If the tower turns out to be of stone, perhaps a carved inscription; if light-colored brick, then perhaps black diaper work—whatever it takes to provide the necessary "sparkle."

This is how the *parti* of the tower might have been handled, but indication could tell the architect how to handle smaller details as well. One example: at the angle of the tower nearest us, the continuity of smooth surface from corner pier to arcade wall serves to tie the tower to the arcade, but because of this arrangement, there is so much uninterrupted white that the eye rises too quickly up the re-entrant corner. Some dark spot is needed to slow and divert that movement. Perhaps an aedicule will do it, or a pinnacle on a squinch arch? Indication can even tell where to plant trees: the two at the right provide the dark against light that carries the eye over to the arcade leading to the tower.

Indication was used to study the visual effects of materials, too. Guptill gives a series of techniques for capturing the effects of light falling on certain materials (figures 15, 16), and one can see these techniques used again and again, almost as a vocabulary, for deciding (for example) whether shingles or slates would give a roof the visual effect needed. There are even cases in which the studying goes beyond these standardized techniques and the architect tries, in his materials, to capture the quality of the ink or pencil line itself. Turn back to Guptill's favored ways of laying down a uniform tone (figure 6) and look at example number five. Then compare that technique with the handling of the low brick wall in Schell Lewis's rendering (figure 17) and with the vogue (prevalent in Tudor houses) for highly textured brick walls with accents of twisted bricks.

Here we see what it means truly to engage the influenced audience. The architect was able, purely by the force of his forms upon their expectations, to influence the preferences of his audience. The wall in the picture looks so "right" that, even if he had never seen such a wall in real life, the client would want the architect to build him a

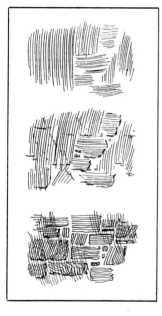

Figure 15. Sketches by Guptill of a technique for rendering stonework show how to (1) cover the area with a tone, (2) add accents, and (3) complete by adding crosshatching.

Figure 16. Sketches by Guptill of techniques for rendering other materials.

Figure 17. Rendering by Schell
Lewis of a house by Alfred
Cookman Cass.

wall like that one. The architect engaged his audience and brought them, honestly and without coercion, to want what he wanted.

But we no longer choose to build this way. Why is that? It certainly is not because our conception of what makes a good picture has changed substantially. Any look at the newest drawing handbooks will show that the qualities Ruskin and Guptill touted are still being taught. We still like those qualities of breadth, contrast, and focus. Why did we stop putting them in our buildings?

An answer to the question can be found by looking at the convention of greeting. In America, today, we greet each other by a conventionalized process in which I extend my hand and ask something like, "How are you?" and you take my hand and reply, "Fine, thanks." We could greet each other in any number of other ways, but we prefer to do it this way. To us, it feels right. In fact, we keep doing it this way largely because we find that whenever we greet people in this way we feel at ease with them. Being able to feel at ease is our reason for wanting it to be this way and not some other. The problem, though, is that, desirable as feeling at ease with someone might be, if we do not go on with the person to establish a deeper basis for our companionability, the conventions of greeting eventually come to feel strained, unnatural, and, finally, unsatisfying. That is, you and I exchange the conventional pleasantries in the hope and belief that we will find we share values more important than our shared acceptance of the greeting gesture. But if our conversation reveals to us that there is nothing else that we share, we realize that our belief was false and our companionability had no real basis, and so we part from each other feeling let down. From that point on, any ease engendered by subsequent greetings will be tainted because we know it to be a sham. Even the memory of the untainted ease we felt in our first encounter comes now to be tinged, revoked, as it were, by our present realization that that feeling was hollow, baseless.

I think it fair to say that the analogous convention of seeing buildings as pictures came to feel unsatisfying because it failed to establish a deeper basis for liking the buildings. When we find that we like the way a building looks, we examine it in the hope and belief that it will reflect values more important to us than visual delight. But the more we examine the Scenographic buildings (the more we learn the ways in which visual delight has been produced for us), the more we become aware that, too often, that is all there is. The buildings do not tell us of values that are deeper and more important to us. They are purely and only machines for producing visual delight. Once this idea enters our consciousness, we find that our delight is tinged with dissatisfaction. The forms that once ingratiated now seem to smirk. The satisfaction they provided now seems thin.

In effect, we feel we now know all that can be known about the building. And with that realization, the building comes to seem small, inadequate: we have grown in wisdom and it hasn't kept up. We come to feel larger than the situation and so feel outside of the situation. Looking back at it, we become aware of how "set up" the situation is, how easily it could have been otherwise, until finally this awareness of inadequacy and arbitrariness blots out the satisfaction we once felt so strongly.

This is the lesson of the Scenographic style—that in order to keep feeling "inside" a conventional situation, we have to be able continually to renew the basis upon which it satisfies us. We have to be able to find new, previously unglimpsed reasons for wanting it to be this way. We have to be able to take the material that is really there, and from that construct reasons for wanting the material to be the way it is. It is this continual constructing of new reasons that keeps conventions satisfying. Our satisfaction is rooted in an implicit belief that we will never touch bottom, that we will always be able to go to what is there and fabricate a new reason for wanting it to be that way. It is only when we go to what is there and find that we can't construct a reason that the convention ceases to satisfy, our satisfaction vitiated by an awareness, which we are unable to evade, of how partial, how arbitrary the convention really was.

People couldn't find new reasons when they went to what was there in the Scenographic buildings, and they couldn't because of the visual, pictorial way the buildings were formed.

But there are ways of forming that ensure that people will be able to find new reasons. I would like to acquaint you with these by showing three conventional, could-have-been-otherwise situations in which people are able continually to find new reasons for wanting the situation to be the way it is. The first of these occurs in games.

Chapter Two

Games as a Model
for an Architecture of Convention

The sportswriter, Heywood Hale Broun, has said of games:

It has always been interesting to me that small children, more than their elders, demand a structure of immutable rules in their games. These kids, given a playground, a meadow, or a stretch of street free of parked cars, will at once begin to create a new sport based on the relationships of trees, posts, benches or whatever and the availability and shape of objects to be thrown, kicked, pushed, or dragged through the mud.

When the code is complete and the sides chosen, woe to the child who makes an aberrant move in the subsequent game. There are cries of, "You can't do that! It's the rule!" The odd phrase, "It's the rule," shouted by children all over the world, is an impassioned demand for the maintenance of an orderly world.[1]

Now take a close look at the source of that anger. The cry of the children is not really so much because one of their number takes unfair advantage of the others and wins "instead of me," although there is that kind of anger of course. No, to break a rule in a made-up game is an act more radical than mere cheating. Let us look at why this is so.

Properly understood, the rules of a game are not merely a set of prohibitions, even though they are often stated in that form. Taken as a whole they are, rather, a description of a complete and consistent way of acting. When we set up the rules of a game, we construct such a way of acting. From all the possible ways we could act, we choose certain ones, and we make that choice on the basis of a felt internal consistency: each action "goes with" every other action to form a pattern of acting that makes sense to us. When we agree to play a game, we agree among ourselves that we will do only those chosen actions.

Seeing children's games in this light, we can easily understand the insistence, the near desperation in that "odd" phrase, "You can't do that! It's the rule!" A child knows the reality of a world in which you can't tell what people are going to do (the world of the playground peopled by gangs, even the world of parents and what they do), and sensing the very real possibility of its return at any moment, the child rushes to the refuge of a situation in which rules are in force. For him, a made-up rule is a positive boon, a thing to be sought and embraced. It is this orientation to rules that sounds "odd." We adults see rules not as a boon but as a necessary burden, not something to be sought but something to be escaped whenever possible. We don't feel the near presence of a world without rules. If anything, we feel rule-ridden. And so when confronted with a rule, our first reaction is not to adopt it but to question it. Why should I do that?

But the feeling of oddness comes from another source as well. The spirit of modernism is not confined to the arts but in large part conditions the way we think today. Like the modernist painter, we feel a need to know that what we do is "the way it must be."

If we are conscious that something is the way it is only because we wish it to be that way, then we are beset by doubts—and if that thing coerces us the way a rule does, by resentment. So children's readiness to embrace made-up rules feels odd to us. Before we will believe in something we have created, we want to be shown that there are more reasons for having it be so than just our wanting it to be so.

It is this need for justification that lies behind what Broun calls "the endless positivism of the sports establishment"—that unwitting but still pernicious conspiracy composed, on the one hand, of scientists who "endeavor to explain play in utilitarian terms . . . such as an outlet-for-excess-energy, chance-to-work-off-hostility, means-of-serving-wish-fulfillment, etcetera" and, on the other, of coaches who "will tell you that sports builds character, creates a healthy moral climate, [and] builds bonds of fellowship. . . ."

The motives [he says] for all this somber tosh are clear enough. Scientists abhor the inexplicable as nature abhors a vacuum. Since most pleasures are by their nature irrational, scientists like to find the grit of onward and upward under the foam of gaiety.

As for coaches, it is obviously to their advantage

. . . to pose as saviors of youth, muscular alchemists who can take the base metal of bad boys and produce golden lads, saints who can block and shoot baskets.

To this conspiracy Broun would add the names of all those who see sports as a model for the conduct of human affairs—for example,

. . . General MacArthur, whose flight beginning "On the fields of friendly strife" seemed to suggest that every time Army won a football game, tyranny snarled and went back into its lair.

Broun rejects all of this. There is no way to justify games on such "positivistic" grounds. When we try to fit those standards onto games, we expose all the more the plain fact that games simply aren't able to provide those positive benefits. But there is one thing that only games provide, and that is the experience of play. And what is the character of that experience? At bottom it is the experiencing of a realm that operates the way we wish the world could operate. Playing a game feels delightful because in a game things happen in the way we wish they would happen in the real world but never do. Of course it is we who have made those things happen that way, by the way we have set up the rules and followed them. But play, by involving us so totally, lets us—makes us—forget that fact.

That is why any thoughts about "Why should I do this?" only vitiate the delight. If we ask, "Why can't the soccer player use his hands?" we only expose the fact that play lets us forget: we made up that rule and all the others.

This, of course, is not to say that one can't think about games—one can and in a sense one must (as humans we *do* contemplate!). Just as we did with the Scenographic buildings, so with games. After we feel the delight, we examine those feelings for deeper values. We go to "what is there," what we have experienced, and look to see if from that we can find reasons deeper and more important to us than delight. The point, though, is to construct only those reasons that actually are "there," within what is real about games, the structure of rules, lest we fall into the trap of the positivists and delude ourselves into attributing to games qualities they don't really possess.

What, then, are some of the reasons that are there, within the rules as we experience them, for wanting games to be the way they are?

We can look first at that delight itself. We know how our ecstatic feelings can take on a life of their own, how when left to run unchecked our emotions feed upon themselves, opening up, on the one hand, ecstasy, but on the other, that dark side of us, the "void of the irrational." We have all seen that side of ourselves when, say, we got carried away at a political rally, or when we became enraged at someone we loved. Games, especially sports we play as games, can give us the ecstasy, but as long as the rules are in force, there is a safety net between ourselves and the void. As a team, we can cheer and regale ourselves to exhaustion and without limit, but the minute we begin to abuse our opponents, we transgress the rules and somebody stops us. The rules rein us in, pull us back from the void. They ensure that we will have the kind of delight which, were we to stop and consider, we would want to have. We might even go so far as to say that the rules of a game embody a certain wisdom (which is after all our wisdom) about human nature. The rules recognize that we have dangerous tendencies, and they work to check those tendencies. But the rules recognize that we have good tendencies too, and the rules provide opportunities for those tendencies to soar in all their ecstatic beauty.

But note that the game doesn't just hand us the ecstasy. Games require us to work for that ecstasy, which is another facet of the game's "wisdom" about human nature. In games the ecstasy will have savor for us only when we feel we really deserve it, that we have earned it. Games thus recognize how important achievement is to us—and not just by rewarding it but also by protecting it.

In the real world, so many of our achievements are compromised because we know the extent to which each fell short of perfection or we know of somebody who did the same thing better. But each achievement that takes place within a game is not comparable to any other achievement, either within or outside of the game. There is the possibility of a perfect handling of circumstances that occurred only at that moment, have never happened before, and will never happen again. If my church-league softball team makes a brilliant triple play, there is no real basis on which to measure it against anything done in the majors. That play is safe from being found just a little inferior to another triple play that happened at some other time. In games as almost nowhere else, there is the possibility of the undiluted *perfect* act.

The game is set up so that we have to earn the feelings we aspire to, and the game lets us savor those feelings by protecting our achievements from the comparisons that would vitiate those feelings.

And there are other ideals that games let us experience. One of them is the notion of freedom. Broun quotes Sartre—"a skier as well as philosopher"—as saying that "games are the only area in which man is free because they make up the only area in which he is sufficiently well informed to define freedom." That is, a choice between actions has meaning for us, not just philosophically but emotionally as well, only if we take responsibility for the chosen action. If there is no sense in which we can be both blamed and credited for the consequences that result from that act, then we cannot really be said to be free agents, acting responsibly and with volition. But so often in the real world those are precisely the kinds of choices we have to make—choices in which the consequences will have ripple effects that spread beyond the compass of our control, beyond the limit of what we could have foreseen. Only in games are we in a position to find out all that will happen because we can observe and know all the consequences of our actions. That is, we might not know beforehand which possibility will occur, but we can know the entire range of things that might occur. And because we can know everything that might happen as a result of our action, we have a real basis for deciding whether we are willing to take that action. Our choice is a free choice because—and only because—it is an informed choice.

There is one final way in which games provide a world that is as we wish it could be. In the realm of games, the self is not on the line. It is not the true, authentic "me" that is out there playing, it is only that limited part of me that the realm requires; it is only my knowledge of the game, my skill at the game, and my commitment to the game that is out there. Why is this important?

Richard Sennett has pointed out (in *The Fall of Public Man*)[2] how our modern demand for honesty and openness has resulted in a situation in which we expect to be judged by others on the basis of our worth as authentic persons and not, as earlier ages allowed, on the basis of what we do in the world, the image of ourselves that we construct. Our modern ideology demands a look at the real person behind the public image, our secret guilts, our irrational desires, our unjustified fears; on that real and authentic basis will we be judged. Sennett points out the cruelty of this system we have, without forethought, imposed upon ourselves. But games provide an escape. In a game such questions are not just irrelevant, they are meaningless. It is not just that they don't matter to the game (in which case we could think about them if we wanted to); it is that the logic of the game provides us with no way even of thinking about them. For as long as we are concentrating only on playing the game, we cannot judge each other's authentic worth. As long as we use only the equipment provided by the rules of the game, we can judge only our actions as players, only those parts of ourselves needed to play the game.

Think how liberating this is. Not only do games provide a realm where we can escape judgment of aspects of ourselves over which we have no control; they provide a place where we actually have a measure of control over how we are to be judged. Not only can we choose where we are to be seen (we don't have to put ourselves forward into those arenas where our performance would be judged as poor) but, even more important, in the arena we do choose, we are not bound forever by one judgment. We can improve our performance and so command a better judgment. For unlike the life skills by which our real-world worth is judged, those natural endowments that are either given or withheld—beauty, compassion, intelligence, sensuality—the skills used in games are the kinds that can be acquired. Once we find our aptitude, we can improve our game skills by simple effort and determination. Only in games, in short, do we have the power to be seen as we want to be seen. And not that we deceive thereby. We are not presenting ourselves as something we are not; rather, from that set of things we actually are, we are choosing which ones we will present. So not only do games give us the chance to experience the way we wish the world could be, they give us the chance to experience being the kind of person we would like to be.

These then are some of the reasons we could construct for wanting a game to be played in the way it is. Again, they are not the reasons why we play games. We play because playing is a delight, and if we play for that reason, then the delight so consumes our minds that any thoughts of "Why should this be so?" are crowded out. It is only after the game, in contemplation of what we have done, that those questions arise. Then the thoughtful person examines the game in the way he examines a new acquaintance, to see if behind the delight there are deeper, more important values. What he seeks is a pattern—some assurance that in its totality this created thing accords with, says something about, or reveals new aspects of the values he holds dearest. He wants to experience a feeling of rightness about this created thing. It is a feeling we might call conviction.

It is in this matter of conviction that the reasons we can draw from games so differ from those we drew from the Scenographic buildings. Our examination revealed that there were good reasons for shaping the buildings in "that way": "building that way" produced breadth and contrast and focus. And those are, all three, qualities we value—but not nearly as much as we value the qualities that "playing that way" produced for us. And not just that. When we looked to see if that way of building reflected values other than those visual ones, we found that it didn't: we "touched bottom." But with games, we find that playing that way reflects a whole range of our values. Recalling a particular play, we might think of it as an instance of achievement, of freedom exercised, of esteem merited . . . and so on. We can return again and again to our experience of a game and from that experience draw new reasons for wanting the game to stay the way it is. We feel a real conviction about the way the game is played, and that conviction is renewed in us each time we discover a new way the game reflects our values.

But note carefully: all those values are convincing and important only because we consider them to be so. Were we to attempt to gather empirical data to prove them important, the data would neither confirm nor deny their importance. That is the inescapable, existential conflict that lies at the base of all human value systems. We have a human nature that aspires to achievement, feels responsibility, has a potential for ecstasy yet a tendency toward chaos, wants the esteem of its peers. But the empirical world will not acknowledge the existence of any of these things. We seek in the world of facts and data for some assurance that responsibility, freedom, esteem do matter, and we find the data mute.

Games and other systems of convention are one of the ways we humans handle this conflict. Although we never say so explicitly, in a game we strike a bargain with ourselves. We agree, among ourselves, to uphold the "delusion" that our ideals matter. We do those things that will endow our ideals with specialness. We withhold ecstasy from ourselves until we have expended extraordinary effort and self-direction. We consent to hold ourselves responsible for the consequences of our acts. We agree to accord respect to judgments rendered on the basis of performance on the field. That is what a game really is for, for giving ourselves the reassuring experience that our ideals do matter.

But to have to admit to ourselves at every moment that "these things matter only because we say they do" would be debilitating. As humans, we may admit to the bargain on one level of our consciousness, but another level needs to be deluded, needs to feel that these things truly are important, that there is no bargain but that this is the way things are. For this level of consciousness, then, the rules of the game are the instrumentality by which we *scrim* the bargain we have made with ourselves.

Look at this notion of rules as a scrim. Think of scrims in the theater, those gauze walls that screen a part of the stage from our view. We know that with only a little effort we can squint and make out what's behind a scrim, but we don't do that. We know that if we were to make the effort, we'd only find stagehands moving props, people out of costume, a set that discloses part of the next scene—the messy reality that we already know is there. So in a play, we keep ourselves from prying, because we know that we'll enjoy the show more if we don't. We give our complicity to the set-up illusion because we would rather experience that illusion than have the certain knowledge of what's behind the scrim. We could, in fact, define this complicity as a willingness to suspend our demand for certain truth so that we can obtain something we value more than certainty.

Complicity is not gullibility. A gullible person would accept the scrim as a real wall and would not consider what lies behind it. Nor is complicity self-delusion. A truly deluded person, convinced of the realness of the scene out front, would not be aware of the stagehands even if the scrim were lifted. Complicity doesn't ask us to go that far. As the name hints, complicity means meeting the illusion halfway. Complicity recognizes that one part of being a human in the twentieth century is a desire to pry, and that as much as we might want to experience that illusion, we need a little help to keep our compulsive skepticism at bay. The scrim provides that help. It makes the backstage reality just unobtrusive enough so that we can—by an act of complicity—suppress our curiosity about it.

Rules give us the same kind of help in games. By ensuring that every action will result in a fitting consequence, the rules provide a kind of reality—a realm sufficiently believable that, by an act of complicity, we can suppress our knowledge that the realm is set up and enjoy the game for its own sake. *Rules are the scrim that allows us to enjoy play.*

Of course there are risks involved when one gives complicity to a situation. Broun's sports positivists illustrate one of the risks. Those coaches and scientists and generals are so taken by the way the rules reward effort and sacrifice, the way they punish carelessness and selfishness, that they take the rules for the way the world works—or the way the world ought to be made to work. But in order to think this way, they go beyond complicity. We give our complicity when we meet a set-up illusion at a halfway point, when that illusion is coming halfway toward us. We go beyond complicity and edge over into delusion when we go beyond that midpoint, when we reach out toward an illusion that is no longer there. When the game ends, the illusion of the rules is no longer there, is no longer coming toward us. We can maintain the illusion only by reaching past the halfway point.

Let me emphasize that distinction. It is complicity to extend belief in a situation we have set up; it is delusion to extend belief when there is no setup. This is a crucial distinction—especially in art, where we often can't be sure what has been set up and what has merely happened. To believe in arrangements that someone has set up would be complicity; to extend belief to an arrangement that just happened would be delusion.

It's that "reaching out when nothing is there" that Broun's positivists of sport do. They forget that the set-up situation of the game is there only during the time that the game is being played. As Broun puts it,

I think it's allowable, even desirable, to pretend within that time frame set aside from actuality, that what is happening is of overwhelming importance. . . . [Believing this] is quite harmless provided we abandon the belief within a few minutes of the game. . . . It is only harmful when, like some lingering germ from a tropical paradise, it darkens the future.

The set-up situation thus exists, but it exists only apart from real time. But if that is so, then obviously we could not have an architecture of convention set up the way games are set up, since architecture must exist within real time.

And so we come up against the same sort of situation we encountered before: A system showed us a part of what we need to know about an architecture of convention but was inadequate as a full model. We saw how postmodernism avoided the pitfalls of seeking the inevitable, but couldn't show us how to produce work that engages an audience. The Scenographic showed us what it meant to engage an audience, but it couldn't show us how to produce something we could believe in. Now games have shown us that believing in something we have set up will happen only if the setup embodies the kinds of ideals that engender conviction and only if we offer our complicity to that setup. But games can exist only in a special realm apart from real time. And architecture, we all know, has to exist within the real world and be used in real time. Is there another set-up situation as belief-worthy as games that nevertheless exists within the real world? There is—in typography.

Chapter Three

Typography as a Model
for an Architecture of Convention

Any page of printing can be read for its written content, or we can pull back and contemplate the ways in which the page "plays with" the set-up rules of good printing. We can, for example, consider the way the block of text fits into the frame of the full sheet. One of the rules of western typography is that the two shapes should be related. Does the text have the same shape as the page? If not, do the white margins balance and complement the gray text? We can look at the block of text itself. Is it even in tone or is it spotty with white and black areas? Another rule is that the tone should be absolutely even. We can look at the individual lines of type. Is the spacing between words even? Is the spacing between letters even? In good printing they are. We can even look at the individual letter forms. How does, say, the lower-case g look? Are the two bowls connected in a pleasing way? How does the white counter (the shape within the black stroke) relate to the outside shape of the bowl? What shape is the little pothook on the upper bowl?

All of these questions have very little to do with the activity of reading. They are questions that barely enter our minds when we are concentrating on getting the written meaning out of a page of text. They would, in fact, impede our reading if they occupied too much of our attention. But the fact remains that they are matters that can plausibly be thought about, and their object—the thing the thoughts are directed toward—is the same printed page we read. How can we characterize such a situation?

The term I would like to use is *copresent.* The object for contemplation is copresent with the object for reading.

Let us put aside the question of whether they are the same object, or whether one or the other is really there, or whether we are dealing with percepts rather than real objects. Our common sense tells us that the same physical page can be seen in two clearly different ways. Let us simply say that the two ways are copresent. And yes, the system of reading is, itself, conventional in that the significance of words is set up. But surely the agreed-upon convention that the characters *C, A,* and *T* will signify a certain four-legged animal differs radically from the convention that a page of text have an even tone. In some contexts, of course the conventionality of language must be acknowledged; in this context, though, surely we may safely treat it as a fact.

But to say that reading and typography are copresent does not mean that they are equal or equivalent. The page to be read is, in all normally encountered circumstances, necessarily prior to the page to be contemplated. That is, the page is brought into existence because of its capacity to be read. Even if a printer wanted to present an especially beautiful example of the art of typography, he would begin from the base of a legible text. Even if the page were brought into existence primarily as an object for contemplation, the printer would never compose a page of nonsense syllables; he would still begin with a legible text.

The typographer's practice of beginning from a legible text is a suggestive parallel to the architect's practice of beginning his creative work from the base of a usable program. Even when just sketching for his own amusement, the architect usually has some sort of use-pattern in mind. And the reason-for-being of an actual building is nearly always to produce usable space, even in the extreme case of a building meant primarily for contemplation.

But this analogy between use and reading also brings into focus how much the way we view buildings differs from the way we look at pages. Partly because of the way modernist thought has percolated through society, much of the public today would subscribe to the notion that for any given building there is (or can be and so ought to be) a single, perfectly functioning (inevitable) layout. But the entailment of this notion is not only that any design done by the architect is just a kind of superfluous frosting to that perfect layout, but worse, that his designing only serves to distort, to impair that perfection. Some hard-nosed types use this argument to advocate no-frills buildings; others, with pretensions to sensitivity, might claim that the beauty that results from design is worth the price. But both groups implicitly accept the notion that beauty is bought at the price of function.

How different is the way we view a page. In spite of its reason-for-being as an object to be read, we do not even consider the notion that there is one most legible page from which every other layout is a departure into degrees of artiness. We know that there is, instead, a broad range of easily legible page designs, none of them much more difficult or tiring to read than any other. We know too that there is an even larger range of page designs that are somewhat more taxing, but which we nevertheless read quite willingly. We know that we will even plow through a page that is genuinely difficult to read if it gives us something we think is worth the effort. And because the page is seen in this way, in typography the public doesn't see an artistic page design as impeding the page's reason-for-being. Rather, it sees design as adding content to what would otherwise be the bare-bones legibility of a typed manuscript. As long as people can get at and understand that designed content, they will have a reason for wanting the designer to expend effort to put it there.

If we insert the verb "use" wherever "read" occurs in the above characterization, the picture that emerges is one in which there are several, roughly equally useful designs for any building, and the architect, like the typographer, brings into the world that object for use which will most easily allow for the copresent existence of his intended object for contemplation.

I think that this picture more nearly characterizes the way architects actually handle the dual demands of function and intention. I think that as long as the viewer holds onto that functionalist picture of what the architect does, he will so misperceive what is going on in the architect's head that it will be impossible for the two ever to engage. But the example of typography shows us that there is a way of thinking about design that is consonant with the thinking of the designer. It is not a way of thinking that is foreign to us; it is a way of thinking that we already know how to do, a way of thinking we are already comfortable with. One of the purposes of this book is to get us thinking in that typographic way about architecture.

The problem of different ways of thinking arises because typography and architecture are both institutionalized. There is a coterie of people who have special skills and talents, and it is only those qualified people who practice "design." So often we assume that because there is this body of special skills, the viewer and the practitioner will always think in contradictory ways and that the viewer will never be able to understand the thinking of the practitioner. But this is not necessarily the case. Take the example of organized, institutionalized sports.

Even if I don't know very much about football, I can enjoy the color and action of the movement on the field. My companion in the next seat might know more about the game and be able to enjoy the same action for reasons in addition to the thrill of movement and color. And the coach on the sidelines will experience other levels of excitement and meaning. The point, though, is that our reactions are consonant: like Chinese boxes, my enjoyment fits inside that of my companion, and his in turn fits inside that of the coach. The understanding of the practitioner is different from those of individual viewers, but his does not contradict theirs because it encompasses all of them. The understanding of the practitioner does not go against but subsumes the understanding of the viewer.

We saw in the chapter on the Scenographic how destructive it was for the viewer and practitioner to have different understandings. As long as this "Chinese boxes" relationship holds, I do not have to possess the practitioner's skill nor do I have to share his motivations before I can enjoy his work. I can enjoy it for reasons that are important to me, and still the situation will be tenable.

Sports thus give a tenable enjoyment to a person with only a naive or cursory interest. But they also give enjoyment to a person with a questing, active interest.

Each of the Chinese boxes can be thought of as a level of understanding—landings on a set of stairs leading up to the full understanding of the practitioner. It is important that there be these landings because that way the activity is accessible. At every stage the seeker not only finds that he still enjoys the game but he is rewarded for his effort of seeking by a new and richer understanding—an understanding, further, that does not make his earlier thoughts look wrong but confirms and builds upon them.

Typography works the same way. When a viewer says something like, "I don't know anything about typography so I have no idea how the designer came up with it, but the layout of that page pleases me," he is giving voice to a vague feeling that he wants the page to be as it is. If we were to press him, he might examine his feelings and conclude, "I like all that white space around the text—makes it look special." He would then have found a reason for wanting the page to be as it is. And his reason would fit inside—be subsumed by—the larger, more articulate reason of the typographer. Further, if the viewer were the active type and he later found that that page layout was similar to one used and praised by William Morris, the reasons for his pleasure would change, but they would still be consonant with his previous reaction, and they would still be consonant with (because subsumed by) the even fuller reasons of the typographer.

But let me tie this idea to our notions of complicity and conviction. At each new level of understanding, our active viewer encountered a new set-up situation he hadn't seen before. Each time that happened, he could have pried behind the situation and exposed to himself that the page design was only a setup, that there was no real reason why it had to be that way. But he didn't. At each level he extended his complicity to that newly seen setup, held his skepticism at bay, and so was able to find a new reason, a reason he actually felt, for wanting the page to be that way. At each succeeding level he was able to renew his conviction about the design of the page.

Complicity and conviction are thus intimately joined. Each time the viewer encountered a new setup, he was able to restrain his skepticism. Part of his ability to restrain his skepticism was the confidence that doing so would gain him a new and richer feeling of conviction. At every previous encounter the feeling of conviction gained by extending complicity had been valuable—and he expected it would prove so again. Just as on the scrimmed stage, it had been more important, each time, to feel the conviction than to know that the enterprise of page design was a setup.

Do we really do this when we learn about design? Let me present a real example from typography.

When the typeface in figure 18 first appeared in the late 1890s, it won almost immediate acceptance from the public. People liked the way publications printed in this face looked. And when they ordered printing, they wanted their work to come out looking that way too—so much so that by the 1910s, even the smallest print shops carried a full range of this type in their inventories.[1] The point, though, is that the face won this popular acceptance with hardly any of the public being privy to the special knowledge that lay behind its design. Hardly anyone knew the intentions of the designer, even who the designer was. People quite simply liked the way it looked on the page. They found their own reasons, inarticulate and vague but still meaningful to themselves, for wanting the page to look that way.

I stress this point not because such a situation is unusual in typography but because it is almost always the case. A typeface or page layout has to sell itself to the public. The designer has virtually no way of communicating to the public the way he wishes them

ABCDEFGHIJ
KLMNOPQRS
TUVWXYZ
abcdefghijkl
mnopqrstuv
wxyz

Figure 18. Complete alphabet of the Cheltenham typeface.

to look at the face, what they should find there, why they should like it. Typefaces are rarely explained to the public, not in the publications in which they are used or in popular magazines. The typographer knows this and designs accordingly. He knows that he has to engage the viewer's expectations about how a page should look. He puts into the work a reason why a viewer might want the printing to look that way and hopes that the viewer will apprehend that reason (or an inarticulate or inchoate version of it) and come to share it. We will look at how this typeface "offered" a reason; but first, compare this situation in typography with that of new art, which comes into the world surrounded by discussion and explanation. The artist knows this and designs accordingly—to the extent that the viewers of the newest art now expect and rely upon commentary about the work, from the artist and from the journals. The work is not designed to appeal to expectations the viewer already has. It is meant to work upon expectations the viewer will come to have when he reads the commentaries.

So then, what is the "coterie" knowledge about this typeface? Would that knowledge have encompassed a viewer's reasons for wanting printing to look that way? Would it have enriched the viewer's enjoyment of the face?

The typeface is Cheltenham, and when it was first introduced, the typographic community was fully aware of who the designer was, and there was indeed a great deal of comment about the face. Part of the reason for the debate was, in fact, the identity of the designer, our friend Bertram Goodhue ("not a trained typographer"),[2] but there were other, more substantive questions that are still of concern to typographers today. Typographers have always been bothered by both the upper- and lower-case G in this face.[3] The spur on the capital, and the abrupt diagonal in the lower bowl of the small letter—these are forms that the classic faces did not and still do not use.

And indeed, if we in the public step into this coterie concern and concentrate only on those forms, they do begin to look awkward. What, then, does this do to my argument about subsuming? We are supposed to like the forms *more* as we learn about them, not less. But bear with me. We can come to like even those Gs if we carry this study one step further.

Look at a typical page of Cheltenham (figure 19). There is little or no leading (the lines of type are pushed close together vertically), and this arrangement of the type, combined with the visual weight of the letters, produces a heavy, dark shape on the page. This dense look was popular at the turn of the century, and it has its roots in books produced by William Morris's Kelmscott Press. Look for example at a page set by Morris in his own Golden type (figure 20). Morris's pages have a distinctive look, a look that would have constituted a part of a viewer's expectations about how a page should

Figure 19. A page of Cheltenham set for Goodhue's own book of drawings.

Then our chief's modesty was subjected to a shock when the summons came to produce his sketch books and any other material that he might have in the private work room at his house. The little metallic-paper sketch books that we had occasionally seen emanate from this room contained many pages of just such delightful little notes as we had been accustomed to watch him make on the margins of detail drawings; indeed, on the margins of books, magazines, almost anything. Many might easily have fitted a parcel postage stamp without feeling uncomfortable, but were nevertheless complete in every detail. Practically all of these were found to be too tiny for reproduction, however, and so, much to our regret, had to be discarded,—though they were at the same time an inspiration and a discouragement; and our continued admiration of them and attempts to copy them, have, I am afraid, resulted in considerable loss of draughtsman's time to the firm of Cram, Goodhue & Ferguson.

Though it was clear to us all that he was gratified and interested, Mr. Goodhue looked with horror at the number of drawings we, who had collected them, thought should appear, and so, while utterly disclaiming any editorial power whatever, insisted on exercising the right of veto, and reduced the pile to perhaps one third of its original depth. Even now, he tells me, he would feel far happier were the sifting process gone through with again; but as the book is merely a personal record and not in any sense a serious work on architecture or book decoration, he has been persuaded to "pass" the ones gathered together here.

positor. So I entirely eschewed contractions, except for the '&,' and had very few tied letters, in fact none but the absolutely necessary ones. Keeping my end steadily in view, I designed a black-letter type which I think I may claim to be as readable as a Roman one, and to say the truth I prefer it to the Roman. This type is of the size called Great Primer (the Roman type is of 'English' size); but later on I was driven by the necessities of the Chaucer (a double-columned book) to get a smaller Gothic type of Pica size.

The punches for all these types, I may mention, were cut for me with great intelligence and skill by Mr. E. P. Prince, and render my designs most satisfactorily.

Now as to the spacing: First, the 'face' of the letter should be as nearly conterminous with the 'body' as possible, so as to avoid undue whites between the letters. Next, the lateral spaces between the words should be (a) no more than is necessary to distinguish clearly the division into words, and (b) should be as nearly equal as possible. Modern printers, even the best, pay very little heed to these two essentials of seemly composition, and the inferior ones run riot in licentious spacing, thereby producing, inter alia, those ugly rivers of lines running about the page which are such a blemish to decent printing. Third, the whites between the lines should not be excessive; the modern practice of 'leading' should be used as little as possible, and

4

Figure 20. A page of the Golden type.

look. Goodhue's type works a variation on that look—he gives us a slightly different effect. Rather than the completely even tone of the Kelmscott books, Cheltenham tends more toward the effect of a closely packed stack of lines. Once we realize this, we can see immediately the many ways in which the letter forms contribute to the effect—the most striking being the strongly stressed baseline, the line the letters stand on. You can see this baseline most clearly by putting the page to your cheek and sighting down a line of type. Look at how the serifs (the "feet") of the *m, n,* and *h* almost close up to form an unbroken line: their strength and blockiness contribute to that effect. Notice too how the eye shoots past the descenders of letters like *p, q, j,* and *y.* They are quite short (compare the ascenders of the *b* and *d*), and that shortness keeps them from diluting the strong baseline effect. Once we begin to notice these things, we see those awkward *G*s in a new light. The spur on the upper case both adds visual weight to the baseline area and shoots the eye forward like the prow of an old dreadnought battle-ship. And in the lower case, the heavily stressed stroke of the top of the bowl, we now see, serves to reinforce the baseline in the strongest possible way.

Now note what has happened. After a little study into the knowledge of the coterie, we came to see the *G*s as awkward. But with a little more study, we reinterpreted that awkwardness; we came to see a reason for *wanting* the *G*s to look that way. Our second impression, that the Gs look awkward, does not really contradict our third impression, that the Gs contribute to a strong baseline effect. Rather, the third impression encompasses the second, and the first impression as well. We found that the knowledge of the coterie did encompass feelings that we have as viewers. Or more correctly, through the study of that knowledge we found a way to see all three of our impressions as consonant.

We found a way. We constructed a new reason for wanting Cheltenham to look that way, a reason about which we could have conviction. But to keep up that feeling of conviction, we needed the help of a scrim. The scrim that helped us to keep on feeling conviction was the set-up rule of printing that lines of letters have a strong baseline. We could have pierced that scrim, invoked the truth that there is no real reason why type should have a strong baseline, but we didn't. We gave our complicity to that set-up convention—we made ourselves attend to how the typeface handled that convention, and we suppressed questions about why the face should do that. And because we did, we came to feel a pleasure and a conviction about what we saw. This was not delusion. We know for a fact that Cheltenham's letters do indeed make a strong baseline: the set-up enactment of the rule was there, it did come halfway toward us.

In our search for a model on which to base an architecture of convention, each of our possible models has revealed to us more than just that thing we sought. We looked at games as a system of conventions we felt deeply about, and games showed us that we can have such deep feeling only when we can keep ourselves from prying into the setup that engenders it. We looked to typography as a system of conventions that exists copresent with the real world, and typography showed us that we will remain able to keep ourselves from prying only so long as we are able to go to the setup and find there new, previously unglimpsed reasons for wanting the setup to be as it is.

This is the message of the two models: We will feel conviction about the things we create only if we can keep up our complicity, and we will be able to keep up that complicity only if we can keep finding within those things new reasons for wanting them to be that way. Or in its simplest terms: *We will feel conviction about the things we create only if we can keep discovering, within those creations, new reasons for wanting them to be that way.*

Typography showed us how there can be creations in which we can keep finding new reasons, but typography did not show us how to produce such creations. So typography, like games and the Scenographic, is an inadequate model on which to base an architecture of convention. Is there another set-up situation that has all the attributes of games and typography, which will, in addition, show us how to produce work we can feel conviction about? The answer is yes, and the model—the last of our models—is the law.

Chapter Four

The Law as a Model
for an Architecture of Convention

The idea of looking at the law as a model for the creation of architecture is, of course, not original with me. The most penetrating comparison of the two fields (and the impetus for my efforts here) is to be found in Peter Collins's *Architectural Judgement*. In his book Collins conducts a wide-ranging analysis of the total system by which judgments are rendered in order to delineate a complete picture of legal thinking. My focus in this chapter will be more narrow. And because of that fact, I begin with a caveat (which is perhaps fitting in a chapter on the law).

The picture of the law presented here will not be a complete one. When we use an existing system as a model, we are less concerned about reaching a full understanding of how that system operates than we are with understanding merely that part of its operations that helps us with our problem. In this study we will be primarily interested in how judges construct rulings about which we can feel conviction. All the other aspects of the law—how legislatures make laws, how laws are enforced, even how and why the law came to operate as it does—all these we put aside, not because they are unimportant or even because we aren't interested in them but because they don't address our main concern.

The understanding of the law presented here will thus be different from that kind of understanding held by a practitioner. It will focus on aspects that are not so strongly stressed in the actual practice of law, and it will skip other aspects that are central to practice. But it will not, thereby, be an incorrect understanding; it will, rather, have that character we discussed earlier, that of the partial understanding that "fits inside of," is subsumed by, the complete understanding. End of caveat.

I said in the last chapter that the law has attributes of both games and typography. It appears obvious that the law reflects deeply held values the way games do (although how it does so will be discussed later). But can we say that the law, like typography, is copresent with the real world? We saw how, with the printed page, we can just read along without thinking about what our eyes are scanning or we can pull back and consider the look of the page. And we know that when we pull back, we can simply say that the page "looks good" to us or we can list the conventions of typography that are being manipulated there. In a like manner, in daily life we can just deal with each other as we are accustomed, without thinking about our actions, or we can detach ourselves and look back at why we act toward each other in the way we do. And we can then either say simply that it is fair to act that way, or we can list the laws, the codified conventions of behaving, which those same actions conform to. When the law works the way it should, it works so that our vague, commonsense feeling for what is fair is subsumed by its articulated and codified rules.

But as a codicil to this idea, recall the case of the awkward G in typography. It is not necessary that every rule of law look "fair" to our first glance. What is necessary is that, were we to study all or some of the legal reasoning that led to the rule, we would—as we did with the G—come to a greater understanding that would show us how the codified rule really does, after all, follow our standards of what's fair. With our greater understanding (and a measure of complicity), we would apprehend a previously un-glimpsed reason for wanting the rule to be that way. Again, when the law works the way it should, this is the way it works.

But here the parallels to typography end. For in typography, when the designs produced under today's rules of good printing no longer please us, we simply put the old rules aside and adopt a new set of rules that will produce pages we like. We have nothing invested in those older rules. With the law the situation is obviously different. It matters a great deal to us that our laws be more durable than mere fashion. We want and feel a need to believe that they express values that are more than just momentary.

Curiously enough, though, at this point where the parallels with typography run out, those with games pick up. We saw in games how we set up rules that embody our ideal conception of how we wish the world could be. We know how, in a game, we might be tempted to succumb to a momentary desire but, if we want truly to play the game for the sake of experiencing the play, then we are actually grateful that the rule is there, forcing us to hold to our ideals. The rules check the tendencies in ourselves that we consider unworthy and free the tendencies we consider ideal. The law too embodies this kind of wisdom about human nature. When the law works as it should, it holds us to the things we consider enduring and ideal and keeps us from doing the things we consider momentary.

The problem for the law, though, is that there is no absolute dividing line between momentary desire and enduring ideal. Ideals change too, though more slowly. The problem for the law is that every ideal begins as a momentary desire. Now, couple this with the fact that we use the law to save ourselves from what we see as our own worst tendencies, and we realize that there is an inescapable dilemma built into the law. We want it to declare to us that certain behaviors embody enduring ideals; others, only momentary desires. Yet we want it to be ready, from time to time, to take certain of our momentary desires and declare them to be enduring ideals—and because we want to be able to have conviction about the declaration (since holding to it will involve sacrifice), we want the law to do this without ever appearing to pander to us.

Because of this dilemma, the law almost always finds itself at variance with some element of public opinion. Usually this takes the form of the law's appearing to lag behind—an understandable reluctance to commit the law to a new idea until virtually certain that the public will continue to hold that idea in esteem. But occasionally the law will enshrine an idea that the public only later comes to embrace—school desegregation, for example, which we now accept as an ideal. There are also instances, of course, in which the public never fully embraces an ideal advanced by the courts. Busing is perhaps one case of this; but even here the process will shake itself out. Either we will come to accept busing or it will be dropped as a doctrine.

The dilemma is quite real, and it has parallels in architecture. We want our buildings to embody qualities more enduring than those of the moment, yet we want them to "speak to us" in forms that have meaning to us right now. What is wanted in both fields—what the law provides and architecture doesn't—is work that reflects and responds to change yet gives an impression of continuity.

Rather than describe right now how the law achieves this duality, let me give an example from law's history that illustrates the process at work. The enduring ideal that will be undergoing changes in this account is the notion that the maker of an object owes some sort of duty to a person who uses that object. What I will be doing is following the reasoning of the judges in eleven cases that dealt with this issue in the United States and England—the first occurred in 1816, the last in 1932—to see how each judge dealt with the dilemma.

Edward H. Levi has cited these cases (and others) in his *An Introduction to Legal Reasoning,* and when one reads the cases, one can see why these particular ones were chosen. The last case discusses the previous ten; the tenth, the previous nine, and so on, back in an unbroken chain. In each instance we see a judge struggling with the dilemma of framing a definition of the maker's duty that would be attuned to his time but would appear to be in continuity with—or at least not in conflict with—all the previous definitions.

Let us look at the changing conditions to which the judges were attuning their decisions. In the eighteenth century, before the cases begin, most of the fabricated goods that one might buy would have been made by traditional procedures known to both the buyer and the maker. The buyer could inspect the article and assure himself that it had been made the right way. The buyer thus had both the opportunity and the knowledge to protect himself against defective goods. And so if, after he took it home, the article injured someone, the buyer had no one but himself to blame—and the law of the time reflected this condition.

But with the coming of manufacturing, new fabrication processes arose that the buyer could not be expected to be familiar with: the buyer would have to rely on the supplier's guarantee that the article had been made the right way. The law was modified to reflect this new condition. It held that when a supplier told a buyer that an article was safe, then a contract existed between the two of them to the effect that the supplier warranted that the article (used in the proper way, of course) would not hurt the buyer. If the article did injure the buyer, then he could bring suit for breach of contract. But the courts kept one feature of the old setup: if the article passed into anyone else's hands, that person would have no grounds for suing the supplier. It was up to that third person to gain assurance that the article was safe, either through an inspection as before or through a contract of warranty from the original supplier. The legal phrase is "privity of contract." At the beginning of the nineteenth century, only a person who had a contract with the supplier could bring suit against the supplier.

But from the beginning, cases arose in which applying this principle would result in a patently unfair situation. Manufacturing processes and manufactured goods were becoming so complex that a merchant couldn't reasonably be expected to be able to vouch for their complete safety. In addition, goods now passed through a long chain of jobbers, wholesalers. Who was to be held responsible?

So the courts began to construct exceptions to the principle—exceptions that would let them reach decisions that met the current standards of fairness but left the principle of privity intact. The major exception was the "inherently dangerous" rule: any person injured by an article that was inherently dangerous might bring suit against the maker. But again the complexities of evolving life overtook the new rule, and so many manufactured goods came to be classed as "inherently dangerous" that by the 1930s the category ceased to have much meaning, and the principle that the category had been erected to protect, that principle of privity of contract, began to look meaningless, no longer worthy of support. Finally in 1932, a court constructed a wholly new principle that not only made privity of contract look sensible again but dealt with injuries in a way that, to the people of the time, seemed eminently fair. The process continues, of course, and new principles have been proposed to replace those of the 1932 ruling.

Before I show how all of this happened, let me invoke again the caveat I stated at the first: do not look for the practitioner's understanding in this presentation. What I will be presenting will be a partial but not incorrect interpretation of these cases.

Let me also make clear that the kind of law I'm going to be dealing with is case law. For most of the time period covered here, there was little or no legislation dealing with mercantile transactions. When such a situation exists, the chain of decisions quite simply *is* the law. The judge with a new case has no choice but to frame his decision in (what he sees as) accord with the intent of those cases. Many areas of the law no longer work this way. Increasingly, legislation now provides the guide the judge must follow.[1] But the reasoning process the judge uses to decide legislative intent is the same process he would use to decide judicial intent. The reasoning presented here is thus unusual only in its length and continuity. Practitioners, in fact, regard these cases as a textbook example of the legal process at work—all of which makes them eminently suited to our purposes.

Now, at the beginning of the nineteenth century the only person who could sue for damages was the person who actually bought the article. In legal terms the situation is characterized by the phrase, "The supplier *owes a duty* toward only the immediate buyer." *Duty* is the crucial word here. I can bring suit against you for your actions only if it is first established that you owe a legal duty toward me. In the example of a negligent action, the British jurist Lord Esher has said:

The question of liability for negligence cannot arise at all until it is established that the man who has been negligent owed some duty to the person who seeks to make him liable for his negligence. What duty is there when there is no relation between the parties by contract? A man is entitled to be as negligent as he pleases towards the whole world if he owes no duty to them.[2]

Thus the questions that the judges will be concerned with will not be of the type, "Did the supplier act in a negligent/deceitful/irresponsible manner?" Rather, each judge's decision will answer the question, "Did the supplier owe a duty toward the person injured?"

The first two cases establish that there are situations in which the supplier owes a duty to someone other than the immediate buyer.

Dixon v. *Bell*
(1816, England)[3]

(Bell sends his servant girl to bring him his gun, having previously left the gun loaded; the servant girl, playing with the gun, shoots it off in the face of Dixon's son. The court rules that Dixon can bring suit. He does and recovers damages.)

Dixon (the boy's father) contended before the court that Bell's entrusting a loaded gun to a servant girl was the kind of negligent act for which he ought to be able to sue. The court allowed him to bring suit, one of the judges, Lord Ellenborough, "remarking that it was incumbent on the defendant, who by charging the gun had made it capable of doing mischief, to render it safe and innocuous."[4] That is, when a person makes an object dangerous and puts it out into the world, he has a duty to others to keep it from harming them.

An important point for us, though, is the way in which this dictum will be used in later cases. Remember that there is very little legislation, and a judge seeking "the sense of the law" on which to base his decision must find it in cases analogous to his case. This case came to be used as a guide-by-analogy for cases dealing with negligence on the part of a supplier who has a contract (real or implied) with a buyer. Bell, of course, had no contractual relationship with Dixon at all, but he did, in a sense, supply an article that came to affect Dixon, and the court here ruled that in the kind of supplying Bell was engaged in, he owed a duty not to be negligent. Reasoning by analogy,[5] later judges deduced that the sense of this decision was the principle, "Negligence"—that is, "a duty owed and neglected"[6]—"negligence apart from contract gives a right of action to the party injured by that negligence."[7]

The second important point for us is the way that Lord Ellenborough framed the wording of his dictum. He was able to accomplish his assigned legal task—reaching a decision—without addressing the question of the dangerousness of the gun, and so he refrained from doing so. He made his decision no more explicit than was absolutely necessary. He kept it as general, as nonspecific as he could, in order that the sense of the decision could be applied to the largest number of future cases, but also, as a by-product, opening up that sense to future reinterpretation by other judges.[8]

Langridge v. *Levy* (1837, England)[9]

(Langridge's father tells Levy that he wants a gun for his son. Levy sells him a gun he knows to be defective. When Langridge uses the gun, it explodes in his face. The court allows him to bring suit against Levy, and the jury awards him damages.)

It was obvious that Levy owed a duty to Langridge's father. In the words of the trial judge, Parke, "If anyone knowingly tells a falsehood, with intent to induce another person to do an act which results in his loss, he is liable to that person in an action for deceit."[10] The question was, Did he owe the same duty not to lie to a person he had not communicated with (in this case Langridge)?

Parke ruled that Levy did owe such a duty, basing his decision on the fact that Levy knew the gun was intended for the use of Langridge and not the father. On appeal, the court adopted a similar view, "the use by the plaintiff being treated by the court as one of the acts contemplated by the fraudulent defendant."[11]

Thus the existing conception of fraud is not contradicted but is given a new definition. Anyone who sells an article owes a duty not to lie about it, but he does not owe that duty to anybody who might happen to use the article. He owes the duty only to those people he knows will use it. The court's ruling undoubtedly coincided with the feelings of a large number of early Victorian merchants and, conceivably, of a majority of Britons about what was fair. The judge's reluctance to extend a merchant's duty to *any* user reflects a knowledge that the logic of such a principle would lead the law to blame vendors whose connection with an injured party was so tenuous that to place blame on them would be contrary to the common sense of the time.

And so, this small expansion of the existing doctrine being enough to formulate a ruling that seemed fair, the court refused to tamper with any other parts of the law. It refused, for example, to allow a distinction put forward by Levy's lawyer between things "immediately dangerous" and things that become dangerous only "by some further act" done to them (that is: Levy should not be held liable because the gun became dangerous only when Langridge loaded it). But even though disallowed, the proposal was duly recorded and was to be raised again in later cases.

Winterbottom v. *Wright* (1842, England)[12]

(Wright contracts with the post office to provide mail coaches. Atkinson contracts with the post office to supply drivers. Winterbottom, one of Atkinson's drivers, is thrown from a Wright coach and lamed for life when it breaks down because of an undetected defect. The court refuses to allow Winterbottom to bring suit against Wright.)

The way the law stood was that, unless there were grounds for making an exception, a judge had to follow the principle that only a party to a contract could sue. The only two exceptions were those embodied in the *Dixon* and *Langridge* cases. The exception of *Dixon* could not be invoked here because it was not shown that Wright had rendered the coach dangerous through his carelessness; and the exception of *Langridge* couldn't be invoked either, since Wright had not known about the defect and so had not knowingly lied about the coach's condition. Thus, in the words of Pollock's *Law of Torts,* Winterbottom did not "have any cause of action against the purveyor. Not in contract, for there was no contract between these parties; not in tort, for no bad faith or negligence on the defendant's part was proved."[13]

And so, fearing the consequences of expanding the supplier's duty, Judge Alderson stated, "The only safe rule is to confine the right to recover to those who enter into the contract: if we go one step beyond that, there is no reason why we should not go fifty."[14]

The four judges of the court recognized that their decision might not accord with the conception of fairness prevalent at the time, but they felt there was not sufficient disjuncture to justify some new and risky departure. In a phrase that sounds as if straight from Dickens, Judge Rolfe says, "It is no doubt a hardship upon the plaintiff to be without a remedy, but by that consideration we ought not to be influenced. Hard cases, it has frequently been observed, are apt to introduce bad law."[15]

We should also notice two important defense arguments not allowed by the court. Such arguments are themselves interpretations of the sense of past cases, only here the lawyer asks the judge to adopt the proposed interpretation as his own. The judge, of course, need not accept any of the proposals, but they are nevertheless recorded in the summary of the proceedings, available for any future lawyer to propose or judge to adopt—both of which do, in fact, occur with these arguments.

Winterbottom's lawyer first tried to advance a new definition of fraud: When a vendor assures a buyer that a commodity is sound when he (the vendor) is not certain that such is the case, then the vendor has led the buyer into an untenable belief, in effect defrauding him. When this idea failed to win acceptance, the lawyer argued that because Winterbottom had no chance to inspect the coach before having to take it out on the road, there was no possibility of his discovering any defect; that, because of the circumstances, knowledge of a defect was being concealed from him as surely as if by fraud. This, too, the court refused to adopt.

Longmeid v.
Holliday (1851,
England)[16]

(Holliday assembles naphtha lamps from parts bought separately and sells them at retail. Frederick Longmeid buys a lamp that explodes when his wife, Eliza, tries to light it. The court does not allow Mrs. Longmeid to bring suit.)

In his arguments, the lawyer for Mrs. Longmeid, knowing she had no grounds for a suit based on contract (the contract with Holliday was with her husband), sought to bring suit for fraud, for *Langridge* established that when there was fraud, a person not party to the contract could sue. But the jury found that Holliday did not know of the defect; so in the appeal case (this case), the lawyer tried to define fraud on the grounds argued in *Winterbottom*. If the supplier "is not himself the manufacturer, and therefore is not aware that the article is unsafe, he should so inform the purchaser; but if he sells it as secure, he is guilty of a breach of duty, which renders him responsible to everyone who is in consequence injured"[17]—including Mrs. Longmeid.

Lord Parke did not allow this interpretation of fraud, citing instead the definition he himself had advanced in the *Langridge* case. Since that definition allowed one to bring suit only if there was deceit, Parke was still bound by the rule of privity of contract, and he had to disallow the case. But before doing so, he listed circumstances in which a supplier might have a duty toward someone other than the immediate buyer. One instance might be,

. . . when any one delivers to another without notice an instrument in its nature dangerous, or under particular circumstances, as a loaded gun which he himself loaded, and that other person to whom it is delivered is injured thereby, or if he places it in a situation easily accessible to a third person, who sustains damage from it. A very strong case to that effect is *Dixon* v. *Bell.*[18]

Parke thus puts a new interpretation on the *Dixon* ruling, saying, in effect, that the reason Bell owed a duty apart from contract was that the loaded gun he "supplied" was "in its nature dangerous." But Parke does not want to expand too far the circle of people to whom the supplier owes a duty:

But it would be going much too far to say that so much care is required in the ordinary intercourse of life between one individual and another that if a machine not in its nature dangerous—a carriage for instance—but which might become so by a latent defect entirely unknown, although discoverable by the exercise of ordinary care, should be lent or given by one person, even the person who manufactured it, to another, the [supplier] should be answerable to the [recipient] for a subsequent damage accruing by the use of it.[19]

With the phrase, "a carriage for instance," Parke shows how his new principle is in continuity with *Winterbottom*. Wright owed no duty to Winterbottom because a coach is not inherently dangerous. We can say, in fact, that the new principle encompasses the logic of both the *Dixon* and the *Winterbottom* cases—it subsumes them. Because of this move Parke makes it possible to see all three cases as conforming to the same principle. The past is made continuous with the present.

Thomas v. *Winchester* (1852, U.S.)[20]

(An employee of drug supplier Winchester puts belladonna in a bottle labeled as extract of dandelion. Dr. Foord, a druggist, buys the mislabeled bottle and sells it to Mr. Thomas for use by his wife. When Mrs. Thomas drinks what she thinks is dandelion extract, she nearly dies from the effects. The court allows her to bring suit against Winchester, and she recovers damages.)

In this case the judge chose to follow the same principle enunciated in *Longmeid,* ruling that poisons are inherently dangerous, and therefore Winchester owed a duty apart from his contract with Dr. Foord, a duty that extended to Mrs. Thomas. But the aspect of the case that is most pertinent to this discussion is that here an American judge used a string of British decisions as his cited precedents. The British cases were available to the American judge for citing because of their inclusion in published digests of cases. But more significant is the point that citing cases from a British court was (and is) regarded as a perfectly permissible practice. We can see how this would have been so in colonial times, when our courts were British courts, and in the times immediately following the Revolution when the only cases available to American judges would have been based on British cases; but here we are, seventy years later. With the terms we have been using, we can see why such a practice would not disrupt the system of legal conventions. Because our courts kept the basic principles of British common law, even after the Revolution, and because British and American courts continued to make their decisions under roughly similar rules of procedure, our two systems have been (in our terms) "playing by the same rules," even "playing the same game." Or as Lord Atkin said in 1932, "It is always a satisfaction to an English lawyer to be able to test his application of the fundamental principles of the common law by the development of the same doctrines by the lawyers of the Courts of the United States."[21]

George v. *Skivington* (1869, England)[22]

(Druggist Skivington compounds a hair wash that Joseph George buys for his wife Emma; but when Mrs. George uses the hair wash, it causes severe caustic burns. The court allows Mrs. George to bring suit, and she is awarded damages.)

Here, a problem for the court. Commonsense fairness would seem to require that Mrs. George have some recourse, but the principle of *Longmeid* stands in the way. That case established that a person not privy to the contract of sale could sue only if the injuring article were "in its nature dangerous," and a simple hair wash is certainly not so. The only other exception to the rule is fraud, as established in *Langridge* v. *Levy*.

In that case, you will recall, the vendor owed a duty to a person other than the buyer when he knew the article was destined for that person. Judge Cleasby, in this case, seized on that proviso and said that since the druggist knew the hair wash was for Mrs. Longmeid, then he owed a duty to her. "Substitute the word 'negligence' for 'fraud,'" he said, "and the analogy between *Langridge* v. *Levy* and this case is complete."[23] Cleasby thus reinterprets the rule of *Langridge,* stating, in effect, that the salient point establishing duty is not so much the lying as the knowing who the actual user will be.

Implicit in this ruling, although not so stated, is a new, encompassing principle that explains all the cases involving a nondangerous object. It was correct that the wagon supplier be found not to have a duty to the driver, Winterbottom. He could not have known who would be driving the coach. And it was correctly found that Holliday had no duty toward Mrs. Longmeid. The lamp could have been used by anyone in the Longmeid home. All of which is, admittedly, shaky reasoning, and a succession of judges has trouble reconciling the ruling in *George* with all the other cases.

Heaven v. *Pender*
(1883, England)[24]

(Pender, the owner of a dry dock, contracts with the owner of a ship in his dock to erect scaffolding for painting the ship; the ship owner then hires a painting company. One of the company's workers, Heaven, gets into one of the rope slings. It breaks, he falls and is injured. The court allows Heaven to sue Pender, and he is awarded damages.)

The three judges reached the same verdict, but each on a different basis. Judges Cotton and Bowen based their decision on the principle that a dock owner owes a duty to people he, in effect, invites to use his apparatus; so for them, the string of cases we have been discussing did not apply. Rather, they cited a different series of cases involving facilities provided for use.

Judge Brett, however, saw a question of duty apart from contract. But on surveying the cases cited above (and others), he felt that "there must be some larger proposition which involves and covers"[25] the reasoning they display. For Brett, this larger proposition was the concept of *care appropriate to the situation*. He used the example of the situation in which two drivers approach each other on the road: "Unless they use ordinary care and skill to avoid it, there will be danger of an injurious collision."[26] Each driver, that is, owes a duty to the other to be careful. And that duty arises out of the character of the situation itself. It is not necessary, in other words, to show that either party actually knew or thought about the danger, only that "everyone of ordinary sense who did think"[27] about the situation would recognize that the situation itself called for care on the part of the participants. Brett then gives two examples of situations in which a supplier would not have a duty of care. If there would probably be an inspection of the article before use, then the supplier would not owe a duty to the ultimate user. And if the goods were of such a nature that a lack of care would probably not produce danger, then too the supplier would not owe a duty to the ultimate user.

With these exceptions, Brett then shows how his proposition would encompass all the then-existing cases. In *Langridge* (and, by implication, *Dixon*) the need for care by the supplier is obvious. The first exception covers *Winterbottom:* The coachmaker owed no duty because he could have reasonably assumed that the coach would be inspected before being driven.[28] The *Thomas* case (the belladonna) is similarly explained,[29] as is the *George* case (the hair wash).[30] Only *Longmeid* (the exploding lamp) gives trouble, ". . . the case was not brought by other circumstances within the [proposed new] rule;"[31] that is, the lawyer had based his case on the contention that Holliday had deceived Mrs. Longmeid (under either the old or his proposed definitions). Had he instead claimed that Holliday owed a duty of care, then Brett's principle would have covered it. (Not very satisfying reasoning, a fact that Brett's colleague, Judge Cotton, points out.)[32]

Blacker v. *Lake & Elliot, Ltd.* (1912, England)[33]

(Blacker, a bicycle repairman, buys a blowtorch from a merchant who, in turn, had bought the torch, under contract, from the Lake Company. After using the blowtorch for a year, Blacker is injured when it explodes in his hand. He is allowed to bring suit, but on appeal the higher court rules that he has no grounds for action.)

By this time, the courts had come to rely on the principle enunciated in *Longmeid,* that when a commodity was inherently dangerous, the supplier might owe a duty to any ultimate user and not just to the original purchaser with whom he had a contract. But applying the principle was proving difficult, as in this case where, even though they came to the same conclusion, the two judges classified the injuring article in exactly opposite ways.

Judge Hamilton saw the blowtorch as not dangerous. So, the *Longmeid* exception not being applicable, only the merchant who had a contract with Lake could sue, not Blacker. And, just as all the previous cases had fallen into continuity when explained by the *Longmeid* reasoning, so this case would fall into continuity with them. The problem, though, was the *George* case, decided after *Longmeid* and on a different principle. In that case the supplier of an obviously not-dangerous commodity (hair wash) had been found to owe a duty to someone other than the buyer. How to reconcile that case with this? His answer: "When [that] decision has been supported, it has been on grounds which make it no authority in the present case."[34] That is, (with the exception of Brett's opinion) *George* had been cited only as a guide to handling cases in which *fraud* was alleged. No fraud was alleged here, so *George* did not apply.

   Judge Lush, on the other hand, felt that a blowtorch was inherently dangerous, but that a person like the repairman Blacker would certainly know this and so had no one to blame but himself. In legal terms, of course, this commonsense assertion would not be enough. So Judge Lush constructs the following argument. He first sets forth his view of the principle of the inherently dangerous object:

If, therefore, a person dealing with an object of a dangerous nature which he knows to be dangerous hands it over to somebody else who is ignorant of its true nature without warning him, he commits a breach of duty not only to the person who contracts with him, but to all the persons who to his knowledge may use it.[35]

Lush, in effect, takes what was previously seen as a minor implication of the principle—the warning—and declares that to be the principle's salient point. The supplier's duty to all users is not to see that they won't be harmed by the article (as *Longmeid* implied Dixon should have done with his gun), but rather his duty to all users is to see that they are aware that the object can harm them. Once we accept that as a principle, then it only follows that the supplier's duty to make the user aware will be discharged if the user already is aware.[36] Since Blacker was aware, the Lake Company owed no further duty to him, and he had no grounds for a suit against them.

Although Judge Lush doesn't say so, the logic of this principle encompasses all the previous cases—reexplains them in such a way that they look to be in continuity with each other. It was right that Winterbottom was not allowed to sue because, as a coachman, he knew that coaches could break down. Any housewife like Mrs. Longmeid should know the potential for danger in a naphtha lamp—she shouldn't be allowed to bring suit either. On the other hand, it was right that Mrs. Thomas be allowed to sue for the drug, Mrs. George for the hair wash—even Heaven for the sling—because none of those three would have had any reason to suspect that the objects they used were dangerous.

Lush's course of reasoning was not picked up by the judicial community, however, and so the courts kept looking for a way of resolving the problem of the nature of the object. Another attempt was made three years later.

Cadillac v. *Johnson* (1915, U.S.)[37]

(Johnson buys a new Cadillac from a dealer. He is injured when the right front wheel comes off and the car turns over. Johnson is not allowed to recover damages.)

The court in this case decided not to attempt a wholesale reinterpretation of the cases, but instead restated the principle implicit in the *Longmeid* case—but with a slight modification from Brett's dicta:

One who manufactures articles inherently dangerous, e.g. poisons, dynamite, gunpowder, torpedoes, bottles of water under gas pressure, is liable in tort to parties which they injure, unless he has exercised reasonable care with reference to the articles manufactured . . . On the other hand, one who manufactures articles dangerous only if defectively made, or installed, e.g. tables, chairs, pictures or mirrors hung on the walls, carriages, automobiles, and so on is not liable to third parties for injuries caused by them, except in cases of willful injury or fraud.[38]

Accordingly, an automobile being judged dangerous only if defectively made, and no fraud being alleged, Cadillac owed a duty only to the dealer to whom it had sold the car. It owed no duty to Johnson, and so he had no grounds for a suit.

In a sense, this decision crystallized the state of the law at that time, setting forth in explicit detail how one should rule when certain specified circumstances were present. But by being so specific, this opinion boxed in future judges. With its long classification of objects, it would necessarily force out into the open any subsequent attempt to reclassify a named object, leaving no way out of having to admit that a past decision was wrong. Indeed, the very next year, the automobile was reclassified, with a long and detailed decision to justify the decision.

McPherson v. *Buick* (1916, U.S.)[39]

(McPherson buys a new Buick from a dealer. He is injured when the car collapses because of a defective wheel. The court allows McPherson to recover damages from Buick.)

In ruling that the auto was a dangerous article, the presiding judge, Benjamin Cardozo, had to overturn not only the classification advanced in the *Johnson* case but also, by implication, the more venerable classification used in the *Winterbottom* case in which a stagecoach was called not dangerous. But Cardozo turned this to his advantage. He pointed out how conditions of daily life change ("precedents drawn from the days of travel by stagecoach do not fit the conditions of travel today")[40] but the underlying principles by which we live continue, specifically, "The principle that the danger must be imminent does not change, but the things subject to the principle do change. They are whatever the needs of life in a developing civilization require them to be."[41]

Even while overturning the ruling of *Winterbottom* (that a coachmaker owed a duty only to the immediate buyer), Cardozo convinces us that he is bringing the true import of that great decision up to date. He convinces us that he has pared away what is dated and transient about *Winterbottom,* revealing what is essential and enduring about it—and those are the qualities he is following. By casting the argument in these terms, Cardozo shapes the way we see the relation between the *Buick* and *Cadillac* cases. We do not see the *Buick* ruling as an upstart, irresponsibly overturning the older *Cadillac;* rather, we look with indulgence upon *Cadillac* as both an attempt to hold on too long to outmoded practices and as an instance of focusing on the superfluous, the irrelevant. It is the *Buick* case that now seems definitive, incisive. Because the overturning is accomplished in this way, it doesn't undermine our esteem for the legal process; rather it strengthens that esteem by reestablishing that an old principle is essentially fair.

But Cardozo is aware of the problems that the "inherently dangerous" rule has caused (he cites a string of cases in which all manner of objects are put forward as "dangerous"),[42] and he wants to base his decision on a principle he considers firmer. He cites Brett's dicta in *Heaven* v. *Pender* ("its tests and standards, at least in their underlying principles, . . . are the tests and standards of our law.")[43] and then applies to his case both its test for duty and its exceptions. The Buick Company not only knew the car was capable of causing injury (ruling out Brett's exception where carelessness would do no harm), but it knew the car would be sold without new tests (ruling out the exception for later inspection) and used by people other than the dealer with whom it had a contract. "Yet [Buick] would have us say that [the dealer] was the one person whom it was under a legal duty to protect. The law does not lead us to so inconsequent a conclusion." [44]

So Cardozo brings his case into the pattern of continuity I laid out in *Heaven* v. *Pender* and in so doing, brings his case back into alignment with the case "from the days of travel by stagecoach" that he had initially dissented from. Because he could expect a final inspection, Wright had exercised care appropriate to his situation and had therefore discharged any duty he might have owed Winterbottom; but Buick had not exercised the (greater) amount of care appropriate to its situation and so still owed a duty to McPherson, contract or no.

Donoghue v. *Stevenson* (1932, England)[45]   (Miss Donoghue obtains a bottle of ginger beer at a cafe; she pours part of it over her ice cream and drinks it down. When she pours the remainder of the bottle, a decomposed snail floats out. Because of her resulting shock and gastroenteritis, she brings suit against the bottler Stevenson; on appeal, the court allows her to bring suit.)

In this sixty-page decision, five members of the House of Lords rendered their opinions—three for allowing Miss Donoghue's suit, two against. One of the judges holding for the suit, Lord Atkin, felt that Brett's dicta answered all the questions involved in this case, but since Brett's principles had not been received by the courts in Britain, he built an argument for their adoption. Atkin well knew that the principal objection to Brett's dicta was that they were felt to be too widely constructed; but, he said, that was often the case when a judge tried to frame a principle that would reflect current public sentiment. The problem was that "in a practical world" the law cannot guarantee redress to every person the public thinks has been wronged. For example, he says, the law cannot make you "love your neighbor"—all the law can do is to require that you not injure your neighbor. To whom, in law, do you have this duty not to injure? The answer is "persons who are so closely and directly affected by my act that I ought to have them in contemplation"[46] when I do that act. That, says Lord Atkin, is the kind of transaction Brett meant to cover. And to back up his assertion, Atkin quotes from *Heaven* v. *Pender:*

This (rule of care) includes the case of goods, &c. supplied to be used immediately . . . where it would be obvious to the person supplying, *if he thought,* that the goods would in all probability be used at once . . . before a reasonable opportunity for discovering any defect might exist . . .[47]

Thus, says Atkin, Brett never really meant his principle to cover every instance in which a manufacturer put out goods that might cause harm—only those situations in which the maker knew the goods would pass *uninspected* from him to the consumer.

Note what Lord Atkin has done. He takes what, in Brett's dicta, was really a parenthetical example and sells it as the salient point of Brett's principle.

Lord Atkin goes on to show how this reinterpreted principle of Brett explains all the leading cases—but you can, by now, construct those arguments for yourself. More interesting for us are the grounds on which Atkin's colleague Lord Macmillan supports Miss Donoghue's right to bring suit.

Implicitly taking a leaf from Brett (and thus from Winterbottom's unsuccessful argument), Macmillan proposes that the manufacturer has no duty in those cases where there will be "a party who has the means and opportunity of examining the manufacturer's product before he reissues it to the actual user."[48] But he goes on, "It may be a good general rule to regard responsibility as ceasing when control ceases."[49]

With that laconic phrase, Lord Macmillan broaches a concept that really can explain all the cases. Bell's servant didn't know to unload the gun: it was bound to be in whatever condition Bell left it, so he did owe a duty. Levy knew the gun would go uninspected to the son, so he too owed a duty. When he turned the coach over to the post office, Wright's control over its condition ceased, so he owed no duty. Holliday's control over the condition of his lamp ceased when Mr. Longmeid carried it out of the shop: he owed no duty. But the bottle of belladonna was in Winchester's control until Mrs. Thomas drank it: he owed her a duty. And the same for the bottle of Skivington's hair wash: he owed Mrs. George a duty. Pender had control of the rope slings until the moment Heaven mounted them: he owed the painter a duty. Lake's blowtorch was out of his control for a year before it blew up: he had no duty. And both the Cadillac and the Buick passed directly into their users' hands: the manufacturers owed them a duty.

An interesting postlude to all this is the way the two judges have used Brett's proposal and the *Winterbottom* argument. From Brett we derive the standard that a supplier discharges his duty if he exercises care appropriate to the transacting situation; from Winterbottom's argument, that the injured party can bring suit if the transacting situation prevents him from taking actions to protect himself. Both statements were attempts to set aside the standard of the inherent nature of the commodity, and in that sense they have finally won out. In that sense also, the situation has returned full circle to the standard of *Dixon* and *Langridge*. The nature of the injuring commodity is once again irrelevant to the judgment of duty. But Brett's dicta and the Winterbottom argument were also attempts to base the standard of duty not in some objective, extrapersonal inherent quality but in a more subjective notion of personal responsibility. And in that sense, the two arguments have been turned against their own original intentions. By reading new import into the two older cases, the court here is able to show us how they actually support the new standard of duty, the inherent nature of the distribution channel—a standard fully as objective, fully as extrapersonal as the older standard of the inherent nature of the commodity.

I have presented these case histories in such detail because I want to convey not just the facts of the story but also the flavor. I want to give some hint of what kinds of thoughts go through the minds of the people who create judicial decisions—what it feels like to work in this way. In the next chapter I will analyze the way judges worked, breaking it down into methods that could be lifted out of the realm of the law and used to make architecture. In the analysis, I'll be asking three questions:

1. What did the judges do?
2. Why did they do it that way?
3. By what methods were they able to accomplish it?

Once I have answered the questions and marshalled the methods, I will show how two architects, one from the past and one in the present, do work this way, and how they produce architecture that engenders in us all the copresent conviction of the law.

Chapter Five

Methods for Making
an Architecture of Convention

First, what did the judges do?

If we look at the manner in which they constructed their rulings, we can see that they all had a common strategy: *The judges made their opinions plausible by showing how they submitted to the wisdom of their predecessors, but they made their opinions convincing by showing how they exceeded their predecessors.* Further, we can see that the method they used was to cite an older decision and then tell us what the salient point of that decision was. In several instances, the new salient point was manifestly not what the original judge had in mind. But by seizing upon that point as the basis for his argument, the new judge was able to construct a new principle with reasoning that addressed the new conditions but *gave the appearance* of being rooted in the previous reasoning.

The literary critic Harold Bloom has described an analogous process in literature, which he terms "misreading."[1] For Bloom, the activity of writing poetry is an occasion of misreading. He points out that a new poem will appear worthy to us only when we can see it as having something in common with poems that we already know. But if a poet wants his poem to be seen as more than just a lesser restatement of those past works, then he must make us reread those past works in such a way that his new work will appear to us to be the greater. Bloom enumerates six "ratios," six stratagems by which this revaluation can be accomplished in poetry. But the same rereading processes are at work in the law, and Bloom's strategems can be used to characterize the kinds of rereading done by the judges in our legal history.

1. Swerving

In this process (which Bloom terms "clinamen") we see the new work as following the old work up to a point (thus establishing comparability) but then swerving away from the old. But rather than seeing this swerve as a departure, we see it as a corrective. The new work makes us see the old work as misguided from the point of the swerve onward, the new work as developing the ideas along more correct lines.

Judge Cardozo's ruling in *McPherson* v. *Buick* is such a swerving. He compares his decision to his immediate predecessor-work, *Cadillac* v. *Johnson*, and convinces us that the earlier work had been misguided when it classed the automobile as not dangerous. *Cadillac* had followed the logic of the then-existing test for duty apart from contract up to a point, but had gone astray. The *Buick* ruling, Cardozo convinces us, corrects that misstep.

2. Completion

In this form of rereading (which Bloom calls "tessera") we come to see the older work as incomplete, as not having followed ideas out to their logical end. The new work we see as completing the old, developing the full implications of the ideas. Because of its more extensive development, we look upon the new work as more tough-minded than the old, as willing to face implications that the earlier work had shied away from. We are thus not surprised when the implications of the new work turn out to be different from the ones uncovered by the older work.

George v. *Skivington,* the case of the caustic hair wash, is an example of completion. The judge rereads the *Longmeid* case and concludes that ruling has unexplored implications. He points out that if one accepts the principle that fraud is the concealment of knowledge from the consumer, then one must also accept that any concealment, be it deliberate or inadvertent, constitutes fraud.

3. Focusing

If the central ideas of a work can be developed in a misguided way, then we can say that they can also be developed in a diffuse way. This is the reading we adopt under focusing (Bloom's "daemonization"). The new creator shows us how the predecessor-works are unfocused, how they develop their ideas in a way that is so general, so unspecific that they fail to engage our daily concerns. The new work, on the other hand, is incisive, definitive. It states widely applicable principles, but it does so in a way that seems to address specific concerns with directness and precision.

The opinion in the *Cadillac* case does something like focusing. It pulls together the leading predecessor-cases and then shows how the accumulated import of those cases provides a standard of liability that is too unfocused, too unspecific to be useful. To remedy the situation, the new court will restate that accumulated import, but now in a definitive, incisive form. The implication here is that we need no longer leaf through old dusty *Longmeid* or *Winterbottom*; we can go straight to *Cadillac* for all the guidance we need.

4. Self-Limitation

There is one more way in which the development of central ideas can appear flawed. The development might appear to contain elements that are superfluous to the central point. Under self-limitation (Bloom's "askesis"), the new creator sells us on the idea that, by deliberately limiting his development of the ideas, he has cut away the superfluous, allowing the essential to show through with greater clarity.

The *Donoghue* case provides an example of self-limitation. Lord Macmillan convinces us that his simple standard of control is sufficient to the task of determining duty apart from contract—that the standards advanced in *Longmeid* (Is the object dangerous?) and in *Winterbottom* (Did the injured party have the opportunity to inspect?) deal with issues that are superfluous to the central idea.

5. Refilling

The first four modes of rereading deal with the manner in which a work unfolds its central ideas. But we can also look at the total import of the work, the meaning that we come away with after the unfolding is complete. In refilling (Bloom's "kenosis"), the new creator sells us a reinterpretation of this import. He empties out the "core" of the older work and refills it with a new import. In effect, he says, "What the predecessor really meant was . . . ." Accepting this new import, we look again at the way in which the earlier creator elaborated his ideas, and naturally that elaboration now seems pointless, the ideas it conveys, irrelevant.

Lord Atkin's reasoning in the Donoghue case is an example of refilling. There he looked back at all the attempts to establish duty apart from contract via an examination of the object, and said (in effect), "What all those judges were really trying to do was to enforce the injunction 'Love thy neighbor.' All that elaboration about the nature of the object is simply irrelevant to this central meaning. A truer development of that meaning is . . . ."

6. Becoming the Essence

Finally, there is another way in which one can reread a work's total import. The new work can convince us not just that it states the import that was only implicit in the earlier work, but that it actually is the import, the essence of the earlier work. Upon adopting this view, we see the predecessor as an elaboration of the new work: it does no more than spin out the implications of the essential ideas that the new work makes manifest.

In *McPherson* v. *Buick,* Judge Cardozo sells us his ruling on grounds similar to these when he discusses the *Winterbottom* case. He convinces us that the principle he states is the essential idea of *Winterbottom,* and that that case is only an elaboration of this essence; worthy as it is, it does no more than add elements specific to its time and circumstances.

So then our second question. If rereading is the way in which new rulings come into the world, why does it happen in that way and not some other? Why did the judges do it that way?

The obvious answer is that, over time, the process showed itself capable of producing what was needed and came gradually to be adopted. But just what was needed? Two things: first, the public needed law that had enough believability so that they could accept it—that is, could accept its restricting their freedom because of the good sense it made. But (and this is often overlooked) the judges who made the law, being, after all, human themselves, needed a system that would let them have self-esteem.

The path by which rereading meets both needs is somewhat complex. And the complexity is compounded by the fact that it meets those needs on two completely different levels.

That is, there is a level of understanding at which one doesn't really understand what is behind the judging process and simply accepts it without question. A judge with this kind of understanding would look at his ruling and truly believe that he had caught the essence of the law missed by past eras, and he would thus feel a self-esteem that would compensate him for the effort and the restrictions that the process of judging by the rules had imposed upon him. A lay person with the same kind of understanding would be able to accept the restrictions a ruling imposed on him, because he would see that ruling as not only fair but fairer than the law was before.

But there is another level of understanding at which one really understands how the law works, and at this level the process would still give a self-esteem to judges and a believability to lay people, but it would not be of the kind just described. For the person with full understanding, self-esteem and believability would arise from a different basis.

But the two understandings are not contradictory. This is another case where the partial understanding fits inside the full understanding, and so the person with full knowledge understands and appreciates both his way of reaching self-esteem and/or believability and that of the naive person. But this is also a situation like that of the awkward G in which, at a middle-level understanding of the process, a person knows enough of its workings so that he can poke holes in it but not yet enough so that he feels its inherent good sense—which is precisely the point here. You are probably thinking that rereading is, at best, an unnecessary exercise and at worst a deceptive one. So let me move quickly on to show why rereading is not "awkward" but "beautiful."

The larger understanding that I speak of is aware not just of the particular case or law at issue but rather sees the whole context in which this particular instance is located. A judge with this understanding would see his task not as one of formulating a single, free-standing decision but rather as forging a new link in a chain—linking his decision to those that came before and making sure that later decisions will be able to link up with his. For this larger understanding would know that a legal decision cannot stand on its own, like a provable scientific statement. There is no real reason why any decision must be the way it is, and any skeptical prying—or conversely, any attempts at verification with data—would only reveal that unprovability. It is the judge's reasoning that serves as a scrim for us, which veils that unverifiability with reasoning that is just convincing enough so that our skepticism doesn't rise up in us. But the reasoning that makes a decision convincing consists almost wholly of a skillful demonstration of how that decision adheres to principles contained in earlier cases. That is why it is so important to keep the chain of cases intact. Unless those cases are there to point to—and unless they are held in esteem so that pointing to them means something—that reasoning will convince no one.

Of course a person with this understanding would be well aware that most of the public does see each new ruling as standing alone, as the statement of the law, and that most people will simply accept a new ruling on faith in the wisdom of the law and its judges. Most people will not have that questing interest in the law that would lead them to delve beyond that first naive or cursory impression, by the process that I described for typography. But a person with a full understanding would know that accepting on faith is untenable in the long run. And he would know that equally untenable is the parallel situation in which a decision exists "hoping they won't look," hoping the public won't take an interest and examine the reasoning too closely. A person with the larger understanding knows that the law must ensure that if lay people do look into a practitioner's intentions (and eventually somebody will—and in a better world everybody would), they will find not just the say-so of one man but an intact chain of reasoning that will give them reasons for wanting a ruling to be as it is.

For the judge with this larger understanding, there is another, more personal reason for keeping the chain intact, and that is to gain the esteem I spoke of. True esteem is rooted in the freedom-with-responsibility that Sartre spoke of in sports.

We all know that it is not enough merely to put out into the world a vision of what should be and then call yourself blameless if that vision is abused. In this world we can foresee at least some of the consequences of our acts, and for me to say that I can't is both disingenuous and a cop-out. To say "I can't be responsible for what people do to my works" is to prevent anyone from being able to take me seriously, to accord any importance to what I do. If I want to be listened to, I must accept responsibility. But a person can accept responsibility for consequences only so long as not everything can happen—only when there are some boundaries to what is possible. For the judge, the realm of the chain of decisions marks off these boundaries for which he will be accountable. He accepts responsibility for the consequences that flow from his work, but only for those consequences that occur within this realm of decisions.

The judge with this larger understanding thus realizes that his work will be taken seriously only if the realm of decisions is in place, intact. He realizes further that, apart from that realm of decisions, there is really no reason for his work to be at all. Apart from the reliability it provides, there is no reason why society must or even should keep up that realm on which the worth of his work depends. If an alternative system of laws were adopted tomorrow, his rulings would be of interest only to pedantic antiquarians.

To a person understanding all this, the attempt (that we often see in art) to garner acclaim through an exposé of the conventions ("I had the courage/perception to see through the . . .") would be not just pointless but actually destructive. Once a judge fully apprehends how very fragile are the conditions that permit jurisprudence to exist, his primary motivation becomes not the promotion or assertion of his "self" but the preservation of the realm through which he is accorded worth. He comes to see as honorable those works that don't forge new law but that only keep the realm intact—keep up, for a little while longer, the scrim that makes it possible for people to go on believing in the worth of what he does.

Ironically, then, the judge who reaches this larger understanding of his own work looks with appreciation upon the work of the naive creator who merely follows the procedures—work that, at a middle level of understanding, he might have derided as pedestrian. It is thus the judge who understands most fully what he is doing who can freely decide whether merely to interpret what exists or to promulgate a wholly new rereading of what exists—and to see either path as an honorable one.

Perhaps this last point provides the most provocative comparison for architects, for architects feel a tremendous pressure (both self-imposed and imposed upon us) to innovate. We do not accept the two courses as equally honorable alternatives. But follow the reasoning that leads to such an acceptance, and see how close are the parallels.

For example, think how many of the conventions of "good architecture" (articulation, external reflection of interior arrangement) have only the justification of conformity to past practice. And then realize that those kinds of rules are the only ones whose manipulation we can truly bear the consequences of. Our ability to handle those conventions of good architecture is really the only basis we have for commanding esteem, for being taken seriously. And then realize that those conventions, and that ability to handle them, count for something only within a copresent but delimited realm. Recognize that the injunction, "You must mark the turning of a corner," when pulled out of its history of esteemed instances, sounds fully as silly as the rule, "You must not use your hands," sounds when wrenched from the realm of the soccer field. An architect who is fully aware of this disjuncture of realms would never allow himself to be photographed caressing a building model. An architect who has a firm handle on the actual, real-world consequence of architectural conventions would never think them so important as to declare, "Architecture or revolution."

But it is not just that actions like these show up the architect's arena of action for the fabricated thing that it is and thus undermine the public's esteem for architects. There is more at stake here than the prestige of a profession. The more important point is that when people are made so aware of how "made up" architecture is, it becomes difficult for them to go on believing that architecture is worth doing. And people do want to believe that architecture is worth doing. It is just that, alone, they can't maintain that conviction. They need a scrim of conventions that can elicit their complicity.

Games showed us that belief in the worthwhileness of manipulating conventions will wither unless we are continually shown anew that the game is worth playing. In architecture, only new buildings can make that demonstration—new buildings that show by their masterful handling (and reformulation) of the rules how, as Broun says, "how wonderful it is to play the game."

So then, just as a person who understands what a fragile, made-up thing games are applauds any play that keeps us feeling that the rules are worth playing by—so any architect who understands how fragile and made up are the rules he manipulates, would look with favor upon any work that keeps us feeling that the game of architecture is worth doing. And he would be acutely aware of any work that undercut that feeling or opened it to skepticism or made it look foolish. The practical problem here is that few practitioners reach the level of understanding that would enable them to make such distinctions.

The same situation exists in the law, of having to rule out of court (literally) decisions that would provide too wide an opening for skepticism. But the law has evolved a set of procedures, which judges follow, that helps keep such decisions from happening. The manner in which the procedures work calls to mind our discussion of the rules in a game. We saw how, in the heat of a play, we might want to break a rule to gain advantage, but after the game, when we thought about it, we were glad that the rule had kept us "doing what we want to do." Similarly, judicial procedures work on two levels. Just as rules check us when the heat of play blinds us to what we are doing, so for those not fully aware of how the law actually works, the procedures serve as a check, to forestall misinformed or clumsy or even venal decisions. Then for those who have gained that larger understanding of how the law works, the same procedures serve as a reminder, an aid to "keeping me doing what I want to do." The procedures thus work the way the rules of a creative activity must work. They don't burden the most inspired practitioners because they embody what those people do instinctively, out of their full knowledge of what they are doing. But yet, by making those procedures explicit, they show those at the bottom of the field how to do creditable work.

Of all the procedural niceties that have been incorporated into the law,[2] six are especially revealing for us. Let me quickly discuss each procedural requirement, looking first at what it does at its most basic level, that of keeping the naive practitioner on track, and then looking at its larger implications. Following that, I will run through the list again, this time outlining the analogous practice that each procedure suggests for the conduct of an architecture of convention, showing how each practice works in a different way when seen through a larger understanding.

1. When a judge renders his decision, he does so in terms of legal categories. He doesn't say something like, "A person who sends his servant to get a gun has a duty to see that the gun is unloaded." Rather, he says something like, "A person has a duty to render harmless any object capable of becoming dangerous." He couches his decision in generalities, "unloading" the gun is expanded into the more general "rendering harmless," and the gun itself is generalized into "an object capable of becoming dangerous." As a result, the tie between this decision and any future real event will be ambiguous. No one will be able to say that this decision—and only this decision—applies to the facts of some future case.

This characteristic has two effects. First, it means that if a future judge were to be faced with a case involving a gun and a servant in different circumstances, he would not be forced to rule in accord with the first decision if good sense dictated otherwise. He would not have to deny the earlier case, nor would he have to construct an elaborate rationalization to justify not following it. So long as that first ruling were kept ambiguous, he could simply say that it didn't apply.

The second effect of the ambiguity is that the sense of the ruling can be applied to more future cases than just those involving guns and servants. Many rulings can claim to be following the logic of that early case. The generality of the legal categories makes it possible for later cases to link themselves to earlier ones.

2. By couching the ruling in these generalities, a decision thus comes to be stated as a legal principle. We have seen how such principles are constructed. Each principle was, at bottom, a statement of the accumulated import of the applicable cases then existing. Being constructed this way makes the principles in law inherently tautological. Now, tautological reasoning is distinct from what we might call axiomatic reasoning. In axiomatic reasoning, each conclusion is the inexorable entailment of some more basic conclusion that is itself the entailment of an even more basic conclusion; the conclusions thus build upon each other, like a stack, down to the base of one unquestioned "given." With tautological reasoning, on the other hand, even though each conclusion depends on the sense of some other conclusion, there is no primary statement upon

which all conclusions depend. The arrangement is less like a stack and more like a circle of fallen dominoes. But this characteristic of tautology is not necessarily a fault (any more than is the ambiguity). It is this circularity that allows a later judge to select a different salient point from the circle of dominoes. If legal reasoning were truly derivational, he would have to follow the logic of that base "given" even if doing so would result in a ruling that seemed unfair. Tautological principles allow rereading to take place.

Thus ambiguous categories and tautological principles keep any decision from being inexorable. They work to ensure that a judge will not be bound, in an ironclad way, to a previous decision. But it would be going too far to say that the logic of the law is so flexible that it can be bent to justify virtually any decision. Just as the logic of the law is not wholly derivational, neither is it wholly justificatory. On the one hand, one does not use the law to derive, to find out what one ought to do and think, but neither does one use the law solely to justify, to make what one intended to do appear to be a logical thing to do. Back of every legal principle there is some inexorable, necessary truth to which a judge must accede. The point is, though, that the law makes its determination of justice on a basis other than this inexorable truth. To see why this must be so, look at what is perhaps the paradigmatic crime, murder.

There are inexorable, necessary reasons why murder is dysfunctional in a society, but to make dysfunction the sole reason for calling murder reprehensible would lead to conclusions repugnant to our human values. The disruption that follows the murder of a leading industrialist is most dysfunctional to a society, while the murder of an alcoholic derelict in the street can almost be said to smooth the workings of society at large. If dysfunction were the sole reason for punishing murder, the inexorable logic would lead to severe punishment for one murder and praise for the other. But such a conclusion repels us. We want both murders punished. But it is logical to punish both only if the basis for punishing is something other than dysfunction. That other basis is what the law provides. The law gives us a contingent truth. There is an element of objective truth in a legal principle, but we call that principle true for other reasons, reasons that are contingent.

The procedural requirement that a judge couch his decision in legal principles and categories ensures that the reasons he cites will be only of this contingent kind. But the requirement of couching decisions in contingent principles has another equally salutary effect.

When a judge enunciates one of those ambiguous and tautological legal principles, he will (even though he would never think in these terms) be doing his part to keep in place the scrim that allows us to have conviction about our law. That is, the generality of the principle (which flows from its ambiguity) allows us to feel that it applies to large areas of our experience, but this same ambiguity keeps the specific points of that application unclear. Merely to state the principle does not bring to mind those circumstances where applying the principle would feel unfair. And the reasoning gives an immediate impression of plausibility. Only by an act of will could one trace the course of the logic back around the circle and realize that it was baseless.

Again, it is not as if looking behind the scrim would reveal truer principles of conduct. The only truth that the scrim veils is the fact that the world of data back of the scrim is either mute about how we ought to act or gives us an answer that would be repugnant. When we accept a ruling, we are not engaging in self-delusion but in complicity. There is reasoning there, the judge has put it there for us. It is in reaching toward that reasoning that we pull away from the skepticism that would pierce the scrim. It is only by pulling away from that skepticism that we remain humanly able to keep up our conviction about our unverifiable laws.

3. When a decision is rendered, it is recorded in an archive at the appropriate governmental level (these are then published in various digests of current cases—which is how practitioners get access to them). Each decision is recorded without comment. It is

not classified as to what kind of case it is, it is not evaluated as to how good or important a case it is.[3] That is, neither its applicability nor its quality is given an official, explicit status to which future users of the case would then be bound.

And the practice carries over into the individual decision itself. When a judge wants to follow the logic of a particular case and go against the logic of another, he does not go about it by trying to disprove or denigrate the second case. Rather, he distinguishes the cases—demonstrates how one case is applicable and another is not. He follows the reasoning of one case but withholds comment about the reasoning of the other. (In regard to distinguishing, recall the problems caused by the *George* case.)

This archiving of cases makes any case potentially available for citing, and the practice of avoiding comment on cases ensures that the choice of potential cases will be wide. The practice also forces practitioners to "speak no evil" of cases —which of course can lead to abuse, but which is necessary if people are going to be able to accept the demands the law places on them. On a purely practical level, people ought not to be beset with suspicions that they are being dealt with by a foolish or incorrect law. But on a deeper level this practice of avoiding disproving a ruling works to keep the scrim intact. For the reasoning in all law cases is conducted by the same methods.

Displaying the defects in the reasoning of one case would only raise doubts about all the others — the very doubts the scrim works to forestall.

4. The practice of distinguishing is made necessary by the requirement that a judge cite precedents, previous cases, to back up his reasoning. So, if couching decisions in the generalities of legal principle allows future cases to link up with this one, then citing precedents forges links between this case and past ones.

5. But there is in law what has been called an ex cathedra rule: the citations that count in a decision are those that invoke real cases, actual decisions with judicial intent. That is, to add plausibility to his ruling, a judge might refer to an article by a distinguished practitioner in a law review or even in a popular magazine, but that citation would only be in addition to citations of actual cases.

The key phrase here is "judicial intent." The reasoning used to back up a decision is reasoning that was intended to be used in that way. We can see two reasons why this must be so. We have seen the many ways in which misguided actions can show up the fabricated nature of a conventional realm. To guard against such actions, the law admits into the realm only work that has been constructed within all the rules — within all the safeguards provided by these procedures I'm outlining. But equally important is the fact that those actions with judicial intent are the ones for which a judge is held accountable. A judge constructs a decision according to certain rules, and he accepts responsibility for the consequences that might occur when his decision is used by other practitioners. He has reason to accept this responsibility only because he is entitled to assume that they will follow the same rules in their use of his work. But those consequences, the ones within the realm of legal decision-making, are the only consequences for which he will have to accept responsibility. For example, if a flood of cheap naphtha lamps had hit the market in 1852, Lord Parke of the *Longmeid* decision could not have been blamed. He had formulated his decision in a responsible, logical manner, in good fatih, and in accord with all the rules. But Parke must be held accountable both for the aid and the problems presented to later decision makers by his doctrine of the inherently dangerous object.

6. A judge is thus careful about where and in what forum he commits himself. This concept extends even to the single decision. In each ruling, a judge presents what is sometimes termed his ratio decidendi, his "reasons for deciding" as he did. He states or summarizes the reasoning he used, and in so doing he announces or brackets off that work for which he will accept judicial responsibility. But the requirement that he announce his reasoning has two other effects.

First, it makes apparent any instance in which any of the first five procedures have not been followed, and so serves as a check and a safeguard.

But more important, it makes possible the phenomenon of *subsuming levels of understanding*. That is, the first five procedures guarantee enough ambiguous reference and tautological reasoning so that any person with a partial understanding of the decision (the kind one might get from the newspaper, for example) would be able to read out of that understanding an interpretation that would match his sense of what's fair. Following those procedures ensures that something will be there to which one can extend complicity. The final procedure, enunciating a ratio decidendi, works to ensure that, hovering over all these partial understandings that complicity provides, there really is one greater understanding that subsumes them all. Because and so long as a judge constructs a reason for deciding, there will exist at least one deeply valued reason why a person of good will would want the law to be that way.

So then: How can these procedures be used to produce an architecture about which we can feel a similar conviction? Let me describe six ways of making architecture. Like the procedures of judging, they can be used as a primer, as mechanical rules followed without any understanding of why they work; but they can also serve the knowing practitioner as a reminder to keep him doing what he wants to do.

1. A legal decision is enunciated in generalities drawn from specifics. Similarly, the forms of an individual building should not be addressed only to that specific place and program. Rather, the forms ought to be generalized from the particulars of that situation—generalized in such a way that we could reasonably imagine ways in which those forms could be used (or adapted for use) in some other situation. But the generality should not be so great that a person couldn't imagine a tie back to those particulars. We can feel that a ruling about "objects capable of becoming dangerous" says something about guns; similarly, we should be able to feel that a building, though general, does say something about the unique way life is lived inside. We want the tie between architecture and real experience to be there—imaginable by an act of complicity—but we want it to be an ambiguous tie, one that we can't pin down. We can say that there should be a certain slippage between the forms and the way they address the specifics of daily life.

We can see how slippage would allow each person to imagine a way in which a building reflected the particular activity he carried on there. We can also see how the same slippage would allow other people to imagine ways in which the same forms reflected their different activities.

Forms with slippage also lend themselves to being adapted in other buildings; the form that houses certain uses here can be used to house slightly different uses there. And of course once that reuse has taken place, it becomes possible to imagine links between the two buildings — and any others that might already be displaying that same generalized form. Slippage thus provides the raw material out of which we (by our act of complicity) construct that chain of esteemed instances that will give us conviction about what we build.

2. The principle the judge enunciates takes the generalities of the case and puts them together in such a way that they say something that sounds eminently sensible. The work of architecture should systematize its generalized forms in a like manner. The logic of the arrangement of forms ought to make sense to us (perhaps not immediately, but within some reasonable time of study), but that logic ought not to be the type of logic that flows inexorably from one unquestioned premise. It is up to the architect to see that the design is not determined by one binding and unquestionable organizing principle. Rather, the building must have features that are that way only because that way feels right. The kind of logic we want the building to have is one that is (immediately) sensible but (ultimately) self-referential. We can characterize this by saying that

the logic of a design ought to have contingency: plausible on the face of it but ultimately unverifiable—the kind of logic that can be accepted by an act of complicity.

If there truly were one principle that determined the form of the building, then all viewers, now and later, ought to see the building in that light; to do otherwise would be delusion. But it would also mean that the building would have value only to those who valued that principle. The building would "speak" only to them; to other people and later people, the building would speak of things that didn't matter. Just as in law, contingency frees later generations from being bound to one "reason the building is the way it is." It lets them formulate their own reasons for wanting the building to be the way it is, reasons that have importance for them. And still this is not delusion. A deliberate arrangement of forms is there, coming halfway toward them. They can expose the fact that the logic behind those formal qualities is baseless, or they can, by an act of complicity, take the logic and the organization that is there, and out of that order construct a reason for wanting it to be so.

Contingency and slippage have their practical sides as well. Anything that is formed to address one need to the exclusion of all others has limited use when the need changes or disappears. A more generalized form, one with slippage, fits no one need perfectly, but it fits many needs reasonably well—and usually will fit a good number of unanticipated needs. A building whose form flows from a single determining factor is similarly inflexible. We have all seen designs with floor plans painfully wrenched to give each room a favorable solar exposure. An organization with more contingency might be easier to inhabit.

3. In law, the decision itself is officially recorded; no evaluations or interpretations are indelibly attached that might bind a future reinterpreter. The lesson for architects here is, Do not make too explicit why you did what you did. Keep your intentions implicit and thus leave open the widest possible range of opportunities for future architects to reinterpret those intentions.

Here we are brought up against the art-historical conflict between the desire to have freedom in what you can read into an artwork and the counter desire to know exactly what the artist intended. But if we want to keep people believing that architecture is worth doing, then we can see which side we must favor. That is, however desirable it might be from an art-historical perspective to know why the architect gave each piece of the building the form he did, if such an interpretation were enforced (either through veneration or pedantry), the resulting situation would prevent any future generation from imbuing any part of that building with its own values. It might even be said that such a building would cease to be architecture at all. Certainly it would have ceased to

5. But recall what was said in the law about responsible actions. It is not enough simply to put something out into the world and then hold yourself blameless for how people use it. To be taken seriously (and, on a practical level, to be granted the power to act), you must in some way accept responsibility for the consequences of your acts. If an architect is going to invoke past buildings to support what he does, he takes on the responsibility for what he invokes. It is up to him to see that the works likely to come to a person's mind are works that that person could read as having a comparable intent. It is up to the designer to see that the activity of rereading *works* for the viewer. The viewer should be able to hold aspects of the old and the new buildings in his mind and imagine analogies between them that are resonant, not absurd or discordant. We are not talking here only about the rarefied experience of a building as an aesthetic entity. We are also talking about analogies on more basic levels—analogies between the feeling of this roof and the feeling of the roof of the house I was born in—analogies that give to parts of experience connections that make human sense. These are insights and experiences that only architecture, the art that is used, can provide. They are, in fact, precisely what constitute that stream of people that flow past a building in history. Only when a person has such an experience can a building really be said to *engage* him;

otherwise, it is as if he had passed by the building without ever touching it, or having it touch him.

So the possibility of apprehending these analogies is the product the architect offers to society. He is the only one who can offer the product, he is the only one who can keep offering fresh evidence that the product is worthwhile, that "doing architecture" (as opposed to just building buildings) is worth doing. That is, he must, for himself and for history, exercise some guidance over the quality of that experience; he must, for himself and for architecture, see that when the active, questing viewer examines the building, he will find there a deeply important reason for being glad that that piece of architecture was done the way it was. How can the architect possibly do that?

The answer of course is that he can't guarantee the quality of a viewer's experience. Like typefaces, buildings come into the world without a handbook telling how to look at them. No outside force is going to be there on the scene to prevent a person from wrenching some part of the building out of its intended context and reading into that part an analogy that is discordant or absurd. Nothing will ensure that that will not happen. The real question is, Will a person who wants to have an enriching experience be able to take the material that is there, in the forms, and from that construct an interpretation of the building that in some way fits inside the fullest understanding of the building? Can the architect do that?

6. We can answer that by taking a closer look at the reasoning the judge puts forth to explain why he ruled as he did, his ratio decidendi. When we took such a closer look at games, we saw that games can be thought of as a bargain people strike with themselves in order to be able to experience certain ideals. A close look here shows that the institutionalized system of judging can be thought of as a similar bargain. We in society want to believe that there is such a thing as fairness, but we know we can't prove that such ideals exist, so we strike a bargain with the judge. We appoint him the person who makes up and manipulates the terms and principles of the law, and what we expect in return for this privilege is a scrim of rules specifically attuned to us, one that will deflect our own particular brand of skepticism. We know that if the scrim of rules has a hole, we will feel compelled to pick at it and so expose ourselves to the unwanted fact that our cherished ideals are indefensible. We know that, because of the way we are, we need a reasoning that is "seamless." That is the judge's job—to construct a set of rules without contradiction.

The judge is not doing that job if in his ruling he implicitly says something like, "If I follow the legal principle of _____, my ruling will conflict with what we think of as fair, so for this case I'll ignore that principle." Nor is it enough for him to follow the opposite course and say, "I know that ruling in this way goes against what we think of as fair, but the principle of _____ dictates that I do so." Either course leaves standing a contradiction that would only beckon to our waiting skepticism. What society expects from the judge, and what those six procedures ensure that he will do, is to construct a full consistency, to bring all the parts of the ruling into alignment with each other: through rereading, to bend some precedents into consistency; through distinguishing, to excise reasoning that can't be brought into line. Working this way produces that "seamless scrim," that pattern of reasoning—but it is not just any pattern of reasoning. It is nothing more (nor can it be less) than the judge's conception of what is fair, put into the form of a ratio decidendi that keeps us from having to name and confront the ideal itself. It is this characteristic that guides the experience of the complicitous reader. No matter which portion of the decision the reader picks, he will find in that portion a constructed exposition of reasoning that supports, fits inside of, a thought-out and fully realized conception of what is fair.

Every step of this notion can be applied by analogy to formulate the relation that ought to exist between architects and society. We in society want to be able to believe in ideals about the places we inhabit, but we know that such ideals are indefensible. So society (we can say) strikes a bargain with the architect. We appoint him the person who makes up and manipulates the conventions of form, the rules of good building. In return for that privilege, we expect a scrim of such conventions, specifically constructed with us in mind, seamless enough to thwart our own peculiarly modern skepticism. The architect's job is, in each building, to give form to a set of conventions without contradiction.

Just as it was for the judge, it is not enough for the architect to say, "This facade looks odd, but the principle of external expression forces me to arrange the windows in that way." Nor is it enough to say, "I can't make this facade look good without violating the principle of external expression, so in this one building I'll ignore that principle." Neither course is enough. The architect can't have *either* the convention or the look; he must give us both. We hold in our heads a loose conception of what constitutes an acceptable facade, and we also hold in our minds the idea that a building's outside should reflect its inside. But either of the courses mentioned lets stand a contradiction between those two ideas, a contradiction that exposes not just those two conventions to skepticism but invites doubts about all conventions of form. What the architect must do, in this case, is either make a pleasing window pattern appear to express the interior in some previously unseen way or else use his forms to acknowledge that convention (perhaps by following it in another part of the building) but convince us that it ought not to be applied — convince us that we would not want it to be applied — in this place. Through rereading he bends some conventions into consistency; through distinguishing he divorces his building from conventions that can't be bent into alignment. He does this until every arrangement, every configuration, has an apparent reason for being that way that is not contradicted or undercut, either by other configurations in the building or by any "rules of good building" that we accept. He puts together an assembly of conventions that so go together, that feel so right together, that not only do they deflect our skepticism about why they should be that way, they make us want them to be that way.

But remember that, as in the law, the intention in all this is not — cannot be — merely to present for our delectation an elegant way of bringing certain conflicting rules of building into alignment (that was the failure of the Scenographic style). Rather, the architect has in mind an ideal about how people ought to live, and he has chosen those particular conventions because he sees a way in which he can use them to express that ideal. He sees a way in which he can have every arrangement of form in his building express some aspect of that ideal. It is in this way that the architect can guide the experience of the complicitous viewer. No matter which portion of the building the viewer focuses his attention on, he will find a deliberate setup. When he examines that setup for deeper values, he will, by an act of complicity, be able to construct, from what is there, reasoning that fits inside of a thought-out and fully realized conception of how we ought to live.

This notion of people examining their buildings for human ideals is not as farfetched as it might first appear. People have a sixth sense about buildings that have been designed to "speak" to them. They look for ways in which to read good things from what they see. It is partly nostalgia, partly a desperate flight to something denied them elsewhere. And the readings that come out of such an orientation are rarely, in any sense, analytical, but they are in-context readings, they are plausibly encompassed by the actual intentions, readings for which the architect can bear responsibility. They are readings that produce the kinds of experiences that give people conviction about architecture, make them feel that "doing architecture" is worthwhile. If an architect can get his building seen as that kind of building, then his job is halfway done—the people that use it will, by their complicity, do the rest.

This conception of the architect's role admittedly looks somewhat cramped when placed alongside the heroic mission pursued by the early modernists or the unbounded free play of the postmodernists. But it is a role that is, I think, more tenable in the long run because it represents a fair bargain between architect and society. Judges and society live with this bargain, and architects themselves did so at one time. And when you think of it, the bargain really is a fair one.

If you practice law, or if you were to practice architecture in this lawlike way, you couldn't escape the realization that your work exists at the sufferance of the people. You would know that you have to be aware of what people are thinking because you know they will demand that what you say make sense to them. But you also know that what they want you to "talk about" is not things as they are but things as they ought to be, a high responsibility indeed. And the structure of both systems reflects this realization and impels action upon it. An architect who worked like a judge will study people in their generality. He will try to get a handle on their immediate reactions to things, but he will focus more on their thoughtful reactions. He will be aware of life's aberrations, but he will look for life's consistencies.

Perhaps the metaphor of the glass of water is apt: Is it half full or half empty? From a few surprising and unexpected interpretations of my building by lay people, I could conclude that people are unknowable and that when somebody acts as expected, that's just a happy accident. But from exactly the same evidence I could conclude that people act pretty much in a knowable way, except that once in a while they don't. The first stance is, I contend, too easy. It throws up its hands in exasperation; it is the immediate, facile reaction that requires no effort. The second stance requires an assertion of faith, of complicity. It says that of course the world, as given, doesn't make sense, but that we can make sense of it and we are the only ones who can.

So then—six techniques for producing the qualities of an architecture of convention; six ways an architect can make his buildings engage us, produce in us that feeling of conviction that comes when a building elicits and then supports our complicity. I realize that this format seems mechanical and maybe even a little pedantic, but it is meant to be like the grammar exercises in a primer. With use, eventually the procedures are internalized and our actions become natural; we learn to follow, even override, the procedures without that restricting, distancing awareness that we are doing so.

What I want to do in the next chapter is go through a demonstrative exercise that will show how the procedures work when they are internalized, by showing the work of two architects who followed the procedures without an awareness, or indeed an intention, that they were doing so.

Chapter Six

Looking at an Architecture of Convention

The two works are Thomas Jefferson's Lawn at the University of Virginia and Kresge College at the Santa Cruz campus of the University of California, by Moore Lyndon Turnbull Whittaker. If the prime attribute of an architecture of convention is its ability to engage the viewer, then these two assemblages are preeminently qualified to serve as paradigm examples. During the five years that I traversed the Lawn on my way to classes, there was never an occasion when I was not affected in some way by that noble outdoor room. My experience of Kresge College, on the other hand, was only one long afternoon and evening in the spring of 1974, but images of the place recur to me almost daily. The question to be answered, though, is, Do those six attributes I outlined account in some way for why these two works so strongly engage the viewer? I think they do, and I think the following demonstration shows how.

Let us look first at the Lawn (figure 21). Completed by 1826, the Lawn itself is the space between two colonnaded walkways linking student rooms. Punctuating this colonnade are the ten pavilions. In Jefferson's original plans for his university, the professor for each discipline would live on the second floor of the pavilion and teach his students in one of the rooms at the front of the first floor. At the rear of the pavilion would then be the private garden for the professor and his family. Between these walled enclosures are walkways leading away from the Lawn to the Ranges—a second string

Figure 21. Engraving by Peter Maverick of Thomas Jefferson's plan for the Lawn, University of Virginia.

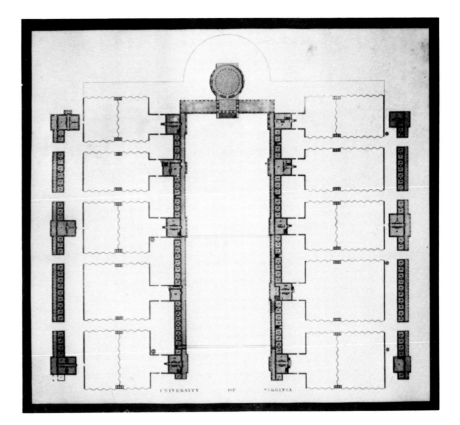

of student rooms, linked this time by a brick arcade, and punctuated by "hotels," or student dining halls, each of which had access to a walled-off rear half of a professor's garden. But the element that clearly dominated the ensemble was the Rotunda (figure 22), the library that stood at the head of the Lawn and looked down the length of the space toward the view of the mountains that lay beyond the steep ravine at the Lawn's foot.

Now the first question to ask about the ensemble is, Does it have *slippage?* Is each of the forms tightly fit to a single function, or are the forms addressed to generalities, the link between a form and its possible uses being kept somewhat ambiguous? Obviously the latter is the case, perhaps the prime example being the "mixed-use" pavilions (figure 23). Their form clearly bespeaks some sort of importance, but it doesn't say just what this importance is. Even when you come to know how the pavilions were used, you still could not make a one-to-one link between a particular use and this architectural expression of "importance." You would be left asking yourself, Were the buildings given architectural prominence because they were where classes were held—or because they were where the professors lived? The question cannot be answered because the forms bespeak only the generality of importance. The pavilions now host other functions—faculty club, president's office—and the unspecific slippage of the pavil-

Figure 22. The Lawn, panoramic view.

Figure 23. The Lawn, Pavilion III.

ions' rooms has made the new fit easy to achieve. But the fact that the pavilions now contain residences and classrooms and offices and a club makes all the richer the answer to any viewer's speculations about why the pavilions are given a special architectural expression. Because of slippage, speculations about what the Lawn "means"—reasons we can construct for wanting it to be as it is—can take on new layers of richness.

Second, does the Lawn have *contingency?* Is there any premise from which the design must flow, regardless of what might appeal to us—or does the design have the kinds of features that make sense only because they feel right? That the second is clearly the case we can attribute to the suppleness of Jefferson's mind. Take, for one example, the condition that the student rooms are linked by a colonnade on the Lawn but by an arcade on the Ranges (figure 24). The rooms in both strings are identical. An axiomatic logic would dictate that they be linked in an identical fashion. But Jefferson did not do this—which immediately raises for us the opportunity to construct reasons about why this is so. There is, for one possibility, the architectural reason that the pavilions, being for the most part columned, would be best complemented by ranks of smaller columns. There is also the possibility that a columned walkway is a more open membrane to the Lawn than an arcade would be—that an

Figure 24. The East Range, with
its arcade and one of the hotels.

inward-feeling arcade is the appropriate face to turn toward what was then open countryside. But the speculation I like best is the one that proposes that since the Ranges and hotels were for students exclusively, an arcade before both kinds of accommodation would convey this condition, whereas the Lawn contains accommodations for two different types of people: students (little columns) and professors (big columns).[1] And the speculations can go on, all of them possible because the logic of the Lawn's design has contingency, all of them tenable because there truly is something there. We are not engaged in delusion, there truly is an intentional, deliberate, set-up situation toward which we can extend our complicity.

Let me move on to the third characteristic of an architecture of convention. Are we bound inescapably only to Jefferson's explanation of why he designed the Lawn as he did? Jefferson wrote copiously on his intentions for the educational program for his university, but his discussions about the architectural form for housing that program are in a style that, fortuitously, opens whole realms of speculation. Those walkways that opened up such possibilities are described in the barest terms, "a covered way to give a dry communication between all the schools,"[2] a statement of obvious fact that forecloses no speculations about the form that dry communication took.

Fortunately too, although Jefferson is revered at the university, his thoughts and deeds are not the only ones accorded homage. This is the inevitable consequence when a building is used, as a living, engaged thing, over a span of time. Events dilute the predominance of the founding era and its artifacts. The student rooms on the Lawn do not still contain the furniture Jefferson intended for them—veneration has not gone that far. But then veneration has not disappeared either: when lavatories were installed in the rooms, each was discreetly concealed inside a period wardrobe.

Fourth, Does the Lawn call other buildings to mind? The answer is yes—the most obvious being the Rotunda, which is a half-size model of the Pantheon in Rome. And there are the pavilions. Jefferson intended them to serve as examples to the students of the best in classical architecture, and thus their designs are derivations of patterns by Palladio and others (figure 25). All this is, of course, in addition to the basic fact that, because they are built in an identifiable style, the buildings of the Lawn call to mind uncounted numbers of other stylistically similar buildings.

But a viewer is obviously not going to speculate about possible associations for every classical building that might spring to mind. In most cases there simply will be no connection, or a connection so trivial as not to matter. But what about the connections that do seem to matter? Does the Lawn call up associations that are resonant?

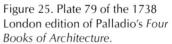

Figure 25. Plate 79 of the 1738 London edition of Palladio's *Four Books of Architecture*.

Figure 26. The Lawn, aerial view.

Let us look first at the most obvious connection, that of the Rotunda with the Pantheon. The Pantheon contained altars to all the gods; it was a temple to all deities. The Rotunda contained books on all the areas of man's inquiry; it was a "temple" to all knowledge. This interpretation leads to another for the pavilions. The patterns in Palladio and Vitruvius were for temples to individual deities; each pavilion was the seat of an individual academic discipline.

And recall further that in an architecture of convention, when we dig deeper, our newly acquired knowledge ought not to overturn our first impressions but instead give them richness and articulation. This happens with the Lawn.

When we dig into the literature surrounding the Lawn, we find, for example, Frederick Nichols' remarks about the Lawn's similarity to the chateau of Louis XIV at Marly (figures 26, 27)—a chateau Jefferson visited as ambassador to France.[3] By the time Jefferson saw the complex, it had evolved into the form shown in figure 28.[4] At the head of the rectangular garden was the chateau of Louis, a center-focused cube. Ranged alongside the garden were twelve pavilions (figures 29, 30), quarters for the nobles summoned by the Sun King, all connected by a wisteria- and honeysuckle-covered pergola. Here again the analogies are resonant. The nobles in the pavilions (figure 31) owed homage to the King; the academic disciplines (figure 32)—even the

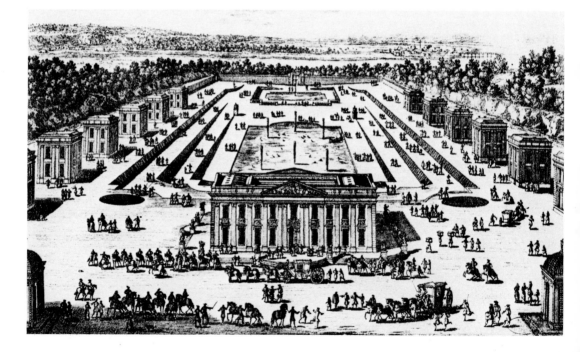

Figure 27. Marly, bird's-eye view, showing Louis XIV's lodge and the twelve pavilions, before the addition of the connecting pergolas.

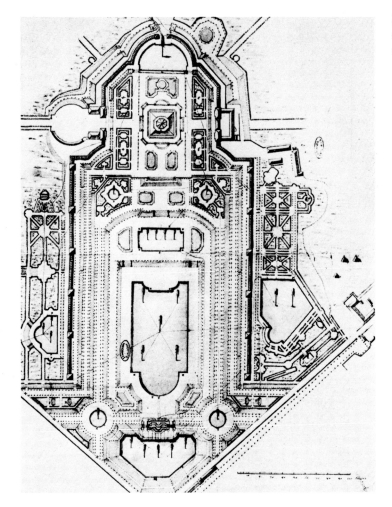

Figure 28. Plan of Marly as it existed after 1693, with the connecting pergolas.

Figure 29. Marly, view of the central garden, with the pavilions visible through the trees.

Figure 30. The Lawn, view with the pavilions visible through the trees.

Figure 31. Marly, elevation of
a pavilion with the connecting
pergolas.

Figure 32. The Lawn, Pavilion VII
and its adjacent colonnade and
rooms in a drawing by Jefferson.

professors—owed "homage" to the knowledge in the Rotunda. And more: Although they had reverted to residences when Jefferson saw them, the two end pavilions had once housed huge globes (figure 33), making them classrooms in a sense—even more, classrooms particularly fit for demonstrating the preeminence of the Sun at the head of the garden.

Finally then, the sixth point, which is really a summarizing of the previous five: Is there, hovering above all this speculation, a patterning analogous to the ratio decidendi of a legal decision, and is the sense of that patterning one that taps our reserves of good will—makes us want the Lawn to be as it is and not otherwise? I think there is such a patterning, and it is this: Jefferson himself called the university an "academical village." Its design is the embodiment of his vision of what college life should be: students and teachers gathered together in the common pursuit of all knowledge. Nearly every relationship of part to part can be interpreted as reflecting this ideal. It is an ideal that ingratiates, tells us that we have a potential greater than our present reality. The Lawn presents itself as a picture of what we could be. Realizing this, we are grateful that the Lawn is the way it is. We suspend our skepticism, we extend our complicity toward the Lawn and actively construct speculations about how its forms reflect and embody that ideal society of scholars.

Figure 33. Marly, drawing of one of the pavilions with the globe installed.

So then, is Kresge College equally an example of an architecture of convention? Let us apply the same procedure.

After an unusually long consultation process, Kresge College (figure 34) was completed in 1972 to the designs of MLTW. Like the other colleges at the Santa Cruz campus, Kresge was planned as a semiautonomous residential college, to contain a good share of the necessities of academic life: student rooms, dining facilities, residential facilities such as post office, laundromat, and lounge spaces, a limited number of classrooms and faculty offices, a readers' library, a gymnasium, and a small number of resident faculty members. In the design solution, the buildings are arrayed as on a spine, following a crescent-shaped forested ridge that rose from the entry point. Several types of housing were provided (mass dormitories, townhouse apartments, loft spaces for communal living), but in all cases the living spaces opened onto continuous covered balconies or grade-level walkways overlooking the meandering communal space. The supporting facilities were then dotted along the length of the spine, interspersed with the housing but with distinctive form or paint treatment to set them apart as special. Finally, the spine itself was landscaped and articulated with watercourses and areas for sitting and gathering.

Figure 34. Kresge College, site plan.

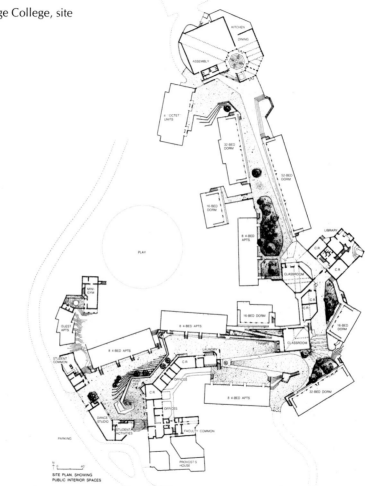

SITE PLAN. SHOWING
PUBLIC INTERIOR SPACES

Given this layout, then, does the design of Kresge have slippage? Does it house its functions in forms that are explicitly fit only for specific functions, or is the link between a form and its intended use kept ambiguous? Kresge does have slippage throughout its design, prime examples being the laundromat (figure 35), where a huge square opening hangs above the entrance, and two sets of phonebooths—one pair arched over by a rainbow (figure 36), another crowned with forms resembling wings or ears (figure 37). In all three cases, the specialness of the activity is reflected in the form of the architecture, but in no case is the activity named. As with the Lawn's pavilions, the only thing that the architecture expresses, in an unquestionable manner, is an impression of a generalized importance. And yet, with all that, we can imagine a tie between the rainbow and telephones (far away at the rainbow's end, two phones linked as all phones are, a spectrum of things said), just as we can connect ears and wings (messages taking flight?) with a telephone. That is, because of slippage we are given the grist for constructing reasons as to "why that form is the way it is," but we are not bound forever and only to that reason. The rainbow, for example, is ambiguous enough to suggest reasons for being connected with plenty of other special uses. If, for example, it had framed the laundromat's entrance, we could have imagined ties between rainbows and, for example, drying clothes (sunny skies, wind blowing clothes on a clothes-

Figure 35. Kresge College, view
toward the laundry.

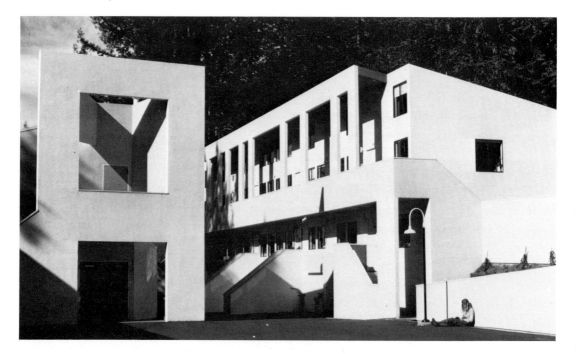

Figure 36. Kresge College, view of the phone booths with the "rainbow."

Figure 37. Kresge College, view of
the phone booths with "wings."

line—even the world drying itself after a cleansing rain; all this in addition to the obvious rainbow of colors that the clothes comprise). The rainbow shares that fecund ambiguity with the temple fronts of the Lawn. The rainbow and its base can, in fact, be read as a kind of Roman triumphal arch, which of course opens up other whole realms of interpretive possibilities.

Second then, does Kresge have contingency? With the Lawn we saw how the design declared its contingency when identical ranks of rooms were given different walkways, not the identical walkways that axiomatic reasoning would require. At Kresge a converse situation discloses the design's contingency. Even though they contain three radically different living arrangements, each housing block is given the same type of screen wall (figure 38), not the differentiated treatment that axiomatic reasoning would mandate. Further, the openings in the screen walls have a syncopated rhythm (figure 39) that has little to do with the widths or fenestration of the units behind. The openings are that way only because that way feels right. We are thus freed and enabled (as we were on the Lawn) to construct reasons about why the openings have the size and the spacing they do. My personal favorite speculation is that the individual screen walls are pieces of a once-continuous thing, and that the window-shaped openings stand for the individual people who can occupy such openings. The different sizes of the openings

Figure 38. Kresge College, view down the central street.

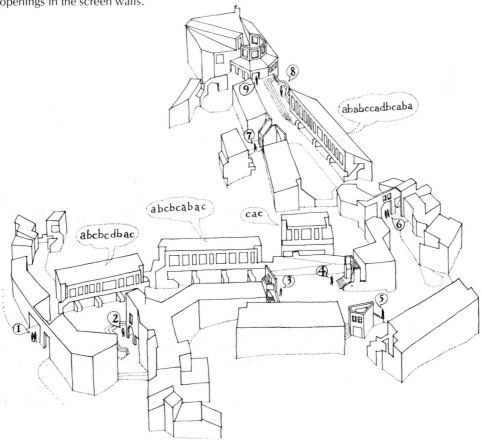

Figure 39. Kresge College, drawing showing the rhythmic openings in the screen walls.

ababccadbcaba

abcbcabac

cac

abcbcdbac

would then express the inherent differences between people, the implied continuity would reflect the inherent continuity between people, but the breaking-up of the continuity would tell of people's equally inherent need to form themselves into groups.

What about the third quality of an architecture of convention: Are we bound to one interpretation of Kresge's design? Since its completion, Kresge has received virtually continual coverage in the architectural press, but there has been a fortuitous lack of unanimity about how the design should be seen. One early comment linked the design with the then-ascendant California counterculture;[5] a British magazine saw the design in terms of its differences and similarities to the work of Venturi;[6] a decorators' magazine focused on the loft-type living arrangements and saw Kresge as an innovative (but failed) scheme for flexibility in interior design.[7] Articles and writings since that time have stressed other aspects, but each has this in common with judicial decisions: Each arrived at a new interpretation by the route of declaring one aspect of the design to be the salient aspect and then evaluating the design on that basis. The fact that the writers could do so—and can continue to do so—is testimony that there is no orthodox interpretation of Kresge.

The architects themselves have participated in this reselection process and thus have sanctioned it (if that were needed). In one context, they show how the design ensures that the spaces will feel peopled[8]—even when not being used the forms themselves will suggest and recall images of people occupying them. In another context the designers stress the kinesthetic bodily experience we get when moving through the space,[9] how the design choreographs our movements to make us constantly aware of the position of our body within the space. Interpretations such as these, then, suggest elaborations of the themes they state and invite speculation about other, unnamed themes.

The fourth question: When walking through Kresge, do images of other buildings come to mind? Nearly every commentator has remarked how the linear space calls up images of streets and squares in Italian villages—or more precisely (as the architects point out) such streets as they are depicted in operettas. But there are more associations than this. There is a fountain set in a partially enclosed atrium that suggests the court-yard of a house in Mexico (figure 40). The shapes of windows and painted decorations on one of the two-story blocks recall the high-roofed town halls of northern Europe (figure 41). And of course there is the triumphal-arch phonebooth mentioned earlier.

But then, Do these images suggest, to the viewer giving his complicity, analogies that are resonant? Yes, they do. Take the triumphal arch: strangers entered a Roman town through its arch, messages from afar enter Kresge through the telephone. And the "town

Figure 40. Kresge College, the
fountain in the courtyard.

Figure 41. Kresge College, the "town hall" at night.

hall": the analogy becomes resonant with meaning when one discovers that the office of the provost is housed in that building. And the fountain—here there are layers of interpretation to be mined. The fountain is enclosed on two sides but on the other it is open to the "street." It is thus a street fountain (as in Rome a place of public gathering like the Trevi) and a courtyard fountain (as in Mexico—a place of retreat from the public). And further, as one investigates the space, the dual imagery is not overthrown but is reinforced and articulated. On one side of the courtyard is a dining hall, which places the associations connected with outdoor eating on top of the Mexican courtyard image, the California patio, the picnic table. On the other side of the fountain is an assembly room, which adds the consonant image of a public forum to the idea of the fountain as a Trevi-like gathering place. The forum image is reinforced when we look up at the pierced tall wall and discover that it is nearly round—a Roman rotunda with the sky as roof. But then we see that the wall is a bright yellow stucco, and we are reminded of Mexico once again.[10]

But the image that sticks in the head is still that of the Italian village (figure 42)—and that image is the key to answering the sixth question, Does the design embody a patterning whose sense will engage our sympathy and so our complicity? When we

Figure 42. A village streetscape at Kresge.

realize that this village is a village of scholars, we realize that Kresge (like the Lawn) is an ideal made actual. It gives real form to an aspiration about what an academy (and by extension, a society) could be. Thus Kresge, too, ingratiates, makes us want it to be the way it is and not some other, makes us want to construct speculations about how it reflects our ideals about society.

We can thus see that, like the Lawn, Kresge College is an architecture of convention, and it is that complex of six characteristics that enables it to work for us in all the ways I have outlined. But we can also see that the key to its success as architecture of convention—the patterning that engages our complicity—is the same key the Lawn used to engage us. Each college gives form to a conception of an ideal society of scholars. We thus have the possibility of comparing the two—indeed, the colleges have so much in common that we feel compelled to compare them. Both are villages in their common intention that nearly all of a student's life could be lived within their confines. Both were deliberately put on sites in the wilderness, set apart from the larger society. Both are organized to look inward to a linear spine. But once we note that the Lawn and Kresge aim after the same thing, the question arises: Does Kresge achieve that aim in a way that is better than the way the Lawn achieved it? Does Kresge give us evidence that we, in our time, are still capable of giving form to our ideals? Does Kresge, in short, convince us anew that architecture is worth doing? We saw that the way a judge convinces us that the law can continue to embody our ideals of justice is to show us shortcomings in predecessor decisions and then demonstrate how his new decision corrects them. Does Kresge do this with the Lawn? Does the built form of Kresge make us aware of shortcomings in the Lawn, and does it then show us how these shortcomings can be overcome?

My contention is that Kresge does indeed do this, does convince us that it embodies our ideals better than the Lawn does, but that it also does this by the rules. It does not seek to "overthrow" the Lawn, force us to disavow our esteem for it; rather, like the judge, it seeks to build upon that esteem by showing us how it merits more esteem. A way of making clear the manner in which this occurs is to use Bloom's strategems of rereading. Those strategems isolate the precise ways in which this garnering of esteem can be accomplished. In a sense, the strategems are like the six questions we have just asked about Kresge and the Lawn. They are a mechanical grammar of the procedures a skilled practitioner or critic would employ without conscious thought. But they can also be used as a framework for speculation.

Each stratagem describes a way in which a new work can cause us to reperceive an old work. We can take each stratagem in turn and look for ways in which the new work might cause us to have that kind of reperception. Where we found such ways of reperceiving, we could ask ourselves if such a conception explained the way we really felt about the two works. Let me, then, go through this exercise with Kresge and the Lawn and see if any of the stratagems can convincingly explain our feelings.

1. Swerving

Under this stratagem we see the two works as handling the same concerns, but the new work's solution causes us to look upon the old work's solution as misguided. We might say that both Kresge and the Lawn are based on the design concept of a continuous, linear arrangement of student rooms but that the form of Kresge's solution acknowledges both the diversity of students (in its three housing types) and their need to form groups (in the separate-but-related housing blocks). Thinking this way, we look again at the Lawn's strings of student rooms, and we now read that solution in a new way. It now appears to express a view that all students are absolutely equal—but also autonomous, without any groupings apart from the whole. Such lonely individualism, we have come to feel, might be a fit model for a frontiersman, but for people living together it is a misguided view. Kresge provides a model that is more correct.

2. Completion

In this strategem the new work shows us aspects we hadn't previously thought of, so that where the old work had once looked comprehensive, we now see it as incomplete. In this regard we at first saw the Lawn as an expression of all that is important in a student's life; but Kresge reminds us that student life—even in Jefferson's day—comprised more than just the room, the library, and the dining hall. Kresge finds ways to use architectural form to acknowledge, even celebrate, those grittier aspects of life like washing, contacts with the outside, transactions with the bureaucracy. Seeing how deftly Kresge gives form to those aspects, their absence in the architecture of the Lawn rankles. Kresge now looks more forthright, stronger—willing and able to handle matters that the Lawn shied away from.

3. Focusing

Here again the old work and the new handle the same concern, but the new work's solution makes the previous solution look vague. In this sense Kresge's linear spine focuses the Lawn. When we see how Kresge's space is articulated with seating areas and gathering places, how the surrounding trees are brought in at certain places, how the spine follows the natural contour of the ground—when we see all this, we realize that this space could be a space only for college students and that it could be located only in a central California forest. It is specific in the way it addresses the situation.

Seeing Kresge's incisiveness, we look again at the green space of the Lawn and note that its form says little about its location in the rolling Virginia Piedmont, much less about how students might use it. We cannot, now, escape feeling that the Lawn has "papered over" the specifics of its situation with a solution so generalized that we can't be sure it really speaks to us. It would have fit a number of other groups just as well, it could have been placed on a number of other sites. Kresge, on the other hand, tells us that it could only have happened where it did, could only be meant for us.

4. Self-Limitation   Under this strategem, the new work does less than the old, but it convinces us that anything additional would be superfluous. One could argue that budget-starved Kresge makes a virtue of necessity through self-limitation. All that it does—its allusions, its embodiments of ideals, its acknowledgment of diversity, its specific address—all this it does with the simplest of means. The essence of self-limitation is effortlessness: Kresge accomplishes its architectural tasks with an apparent ease and naturalness. Once we become aware of this, we look again at the ground plan of the Lawn and realize with dismay the price that has been paid to fit decent rooms into those noble Roman temples.

5. Refilling

Here, the new work convinces us that it conveys "what the predecessor really meant to say." Under a reading of refilling, we might reach a conclusion something like, "Jefferson really meant for the architectural form of the Lawn to express a community of scholars in pursuit of learning, but his design solution of ten different pavilions and many identical rooms more nearly expresses a hierarchy in which an undifferentiated mass of students is ranked below a diverse assemblage of professors. The form of Kresge, in which professors' offices and residences are mixed among a variety of student accommodations, expresses both the free diversity of students and their equality of worth with their professors." Kresge conveys what Jefferson really meant to express.

6. Becoming the Essence

In this final strategem, the new work convinces us that it does more than spin out the correct implications of the essential idea stated by the predecessor. Rather we come to see the new work as the prime embodiment of that essential idea. Under such a reading we would look upon Kresge as the embodiment of all the essential aspects of the idea of an academic village. The Lawn, we would then conclude, is only an example of that ideal. We would conclude that it is the Lawn that spins out the implications of the idea stated by Kresge. Kresge, that is, both encompasses and makes manifest the essence of the academic village ideal: unique individuals seeking knowledge, equal in worth, free to form and reform subgroups, while still feeling an overarching sense of community with the whole.

So then: six possible interpretations of Kresge College and the Lawn. But they are only suggestions. None of them is binding, none is inevitable. Their prime purpose is to widen the range of the ways in which we might tenably experience form. What each viewer has to do, after hearing these possibilities, is to compare them to feelings he actually has about the building—to ask, Do any of these interpretations ring true? Do any of them articulate a feeling I possessed before the exercise? Did any of them arouse in me a realization or a feeling about the buildings that I did not have before? To the extent that the answer is yes, the criticism is a valid interpretation of true feelings.

Recall too that, using the same framework for speculation, I could have constructed six interpretations under which the Lawn would have been judged superior. The difference would be that, for me at least, such speculations would not ring true—they would not match the feelings I feel and so would have no value for me. But they would nevertheless remain possible, potential interpretations—readings which, at some other time or for some other person, just might ring true.

Finally, recall this: To the extent that these speculations did ring true, they recover three aspects of architecture that we had almost forgotten could exist. They show us that architecture can deeply affect us, that there is a way of explaining and talking about why it does so, and that the right kind of criticism can expand and deepen our experience of a building in ways that matter to us. Recall too that only architecture can give such experiences: to the extent that these experiences mean something to us, to that extent is architecture worth doing.

Criticism under an Architecture of Convention

It is perhaps fitting that a book on architecture have a certain symmetry, so let me conclude by closing the circle of my argument, returning to a point I made at the beginning of this book, the feeling of edginess that certain postmodern buildings give. One of the tests of any critical method is whether the criticism produced by that method gives voice to feelings we have about a building. Can any of the critical concepts presented here explain to us, in a way that rings true, that feeling of edginess? Let me offer some possibilities.

Take for an example the stair squeezed behind the fireplace in the Venturi house in Chestnut Hill, Pennsylvania (figure 43). Ascending that stair, we get the feeling of being squeezed between the chimney and the front wall. It's an interesting feeling, but somewhat painful as well. Might not slippage explain the feeling?

The goal expressed by slippage is that form and use have an ambiguous relationship with one another, that we not be confronted with a situation in which a form appears to have been determined solely by use. But that is exactly what happens here. We can't escape the feeling that the shape of the stair is determined by the placement of the fireplace and by that alone. We might even say that here, rather than being linked in an ambiguous way, form and use are contending, struggling with one another. We are so much aware of that connection that we are unable to imagine any other reason for the

Figure 43. Venturi house, Chestnut Hill, Pennsylvania, view down the front stair.

Figure 44. Sketch of the approach to a sign designed by Venturi and Rauch for California City.

stair's being the way it is. The obviousness of that reason prevents us from being able to have conviction about any other reason we might construct (any reason that might mean more to us). Any other reason would seem fatuous alongside the "obvious truth" that the placement of the fireplace is the reason for the stair's shape.

Another view of the same situation is that the stairs don't give us a reason for wanting them to be that shape instead of the shape stairs normally (conventionally) take. The architects have not bent that convention of straightsided stairs by rereading it, nor have they distinguished it. The contradiction—which for the architects has arisen out of the complexity of the program—is left standing.

Other aspects of the work of Venturi and Rauch also give unease. Take, for example, the highway signs for the California City development (figure 44). The designers have indeed learned from Las Vegas in the way in which they combine the large form to be read at a distance (the "high reader") with the smaller signboard (the "low reader") to be read at close range. That much of the design certainly works. But we find we can't divorce that sign form from its Las Vegas roots. Try as we might to suppress them, the sign evokes associations that are discordant: lost money, ephemerality. . . . Is it a tenable situation for people contemplating buying a lot in this development to be confronted with thoughts like these? For it is not as if these were arcane, outré associations that the architect would not have known about—any reasonable person could have foreseen that such thoughts would arise.

A similar situation occurs in Philip Johnson's design for the AT&T headquarters (figure 45). Again the analogies that come to mind are discordant, and any reasonable person could have foreseen them. How is an office building like a grandfather clock? Are we to think of the ascending and descending escapement weights as analogous to elevators? No, that makes no sense. Then perhaps an office tower is like a highboy. Are we to think of the workers as items on shelves behind doors? That connection is not just nonsense, there is a disturbing element of truth in it. But is it the kind of insight that would make us want the building to be the way it is? As a polemic about office work, that kind of thought is relevant, perhaps even salutary, but as an element in a worker's experience of his inescapable daily environment, it is untenable.

When designers at Hardy Holzman Pfeiffer use industrial products in their buildings, they are fully aware of the kinds of associations those objects are likely to call up, but they work to overturn those associations. In most cases their work does do that to us (figure 46). We forget our memories of warehouses, factories, and airport runways and focus instead on the way sunlight plays on corrugated metal, the handsome lines of

Figure 45. Philip Johnson, AT&T
headquarters, New York, model.

Figure 46. Robert S. Marx Theater, Cincinnati, night view of the entry.

industrial light fixtures, the beautiful blue of runway lights. But in less skilled hands, the ploy can be disastrous. An ugly duct can remain an ugly duct even when painted yellow.

Our notion of the seamless scrim of conventions can offer an explanation of why the ploy is so risky. Unless we are deterred in some way, we just naturally find ourselves focusing on an exposed duct and imagining it back in the context from which it came. From the law we took the notion that the architect should allow into the building only those forms that either already supported his building ideal or could be bent to support it. For the ploy to work, the architect has to bend—reread—that duct, dispose it in such a way that it too appears to express his building ideal—give it, in short, a reason for being that way, a reason why we would want it to be here and not back in the warehouse.

This notion of the architect working intentionally to call up associations in the mind of the viewer perhaps explains part of our reaction to Peter Eisenman's houses. They call up almost no memories of other buildings at all. This is, of course, as Eisenman intends it (we are to attend to other aspects of the house), but our inability to connect this experience of a building with any other experience of a building nonetheless contributes to our unease.

But the real point is that Eisenman, by his own actions, undercuts any reasons we might construct for wanting the house to be as it is.

For example, as we use any house, we come to associate each part of it with whatever we might have done there. The piece of wall that hangs on hinges (figure 47) may have none of the conventional appointments of a door, but once we have passed through it, we will, by our nature, think of it as a door. We will reflect on how it is like and unlike all other doors we have passed through. And the same goes for "things that (appear to) hold up things" and "the place where we (happen to) consume food." We will come to think of them as columns and a dining room. We will, unwittingly, establish a kind of slippage between the form and how we use it. We know that the function of dining certainly didn't determine what is in that room (figure 48); other considerations did, but we nevertheless have found a way to use whatever *is* there to dine. By having used those things, we have established that one possible reading of them is that of "things to dine with."

But Eisenman denies this slippage. He wants to deny that any ties exist or can be imagined between the shapes of his forms and their use. Of course if we happened to move into an Eisenman house without ever having heard of the architect, we'd simply imagine our connections and that would be that. But things do not happen that way. We

Figure 47. Peter Eisenman, Frank house, hinged wall section.

Figure 48. Frank house, dining area.

Figure 49. Peter Eisenman, Miller house, view of the stairs to the top.

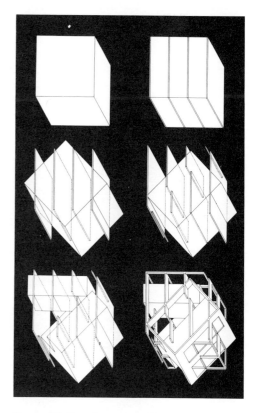

Figure 50. Transformation diagrams by Peter Eisenman showing the generation of the Miller house.

know Eisenman's intentions; he has made them overt and inescapable, in his writings and in his lectures. And for that reason, because Eisenman so forcefully denies any intention to connect form and use, the associations that would feel natural in any other house feel unnatural, uneasy, in an Eisenman house.

But it is not just the vehemence and pervasiveness of Eisenman's intentions that deny us the possibility of easy speculation; it is their inescapable explicitness. In some Eisenman houses the quality of the light is truly enchanting (figure 49), the play of form against form is almost sensuous. But all our feelings of delight are undercut by a nagging awareness that "this is not what I'm supposed to be seeing." What I should be attending to are the transformations delineated in those series of axonometric diagrams (figure 50). By making that intention so explicit, Eisenman makes us feel that any other reaction would be fatuous, baseless. By his explicitness he undercuts our natural reactions and makes them feel unnatural.

What, then, does this kind of criticism say about the work of Michael Graves? Can any of the six characteristics put words to our reaction to his work? The question is compounded by the realization that there are two Graveses—the early Graves of the Benacerraf house addition (figure 51) in which previously unseen forms like that un-

Figure 51. Michael Graves,
Banacerraf house addition, view.

dulant soffit are used, and the more recent Graves of the Plocek house (figure 52), where forms we've seen before are used in unfamiliar ways. But I think we can get at a thread common to both through the notion of contingency, especially contingency as it was used in the law. Recall how the judge was not to take the system and from it derive a ruling. The system of legal conventions was not the kind of thing that could, by itself, generate a valuable creation. It was not enough for the judge merely to "turn the crank," to let the reasoning contained in the existing principles produce their own logical entailment and then promulgate that as a ruling. To do so, we saw, might result in rulings that felt unfair, and rulings that seemed patently unfair would invite skepticism about the whole system of justice.

But turning the crank is very much like what the early work of Graves attempted to do. Architecture (his works seemed to say) was a system of signification and metaphor in which certain forms could be made to stand for certain other forms and concepts. By a manipulation of that system, one could derive new forms, forms that would express concepts in a way not seen before. Thus we might look at the green-painted beam supporting the terrace at the Benacerraf house and see it as standing for the underside of tree foliage, while the undulant soffit in the opening above might call up the idea of a cloud. Putting the "foliage" and the "cloud" together, the terrace would become (in one of many possible interpretations) a kind of treehouse.[1] Upon arriving at this metaphorical image, we would be made aware of how we are able to construct concepts out of abstract forms, even forms as abstract as these.

Graves's early work thus reveals to us how we think. It forces us to confront the fact that our conventions of communication and symbolization are made up, that they could have been otherwise.

Graves wanted us to take pleasure in the contemplation of this fact—and indeed, the knowledge that none of our systems of meaning is inevitable is a liberating idea. It opens up possibilities for whole new modes of signification.

But it also opens up the void. It makes us realize how little of what is meaningful comes from outside ourselves. Graves's work renews in us the awareness of how mute is the world outside human volition.

I think that people sense this muteness. I think they already know what Graves wanted to demonstrate. I think they already know that human meaning is baseless but feel that what we gain when we admit that fact is not worth the price of what we lose.

What about Graves's more recent work? The difference that most strikes us is that, whereas the earlier work contained forms unfamiliar to us, the new work is filled with forms that we have seen in buildings before, like keystones, pediments, latticework.

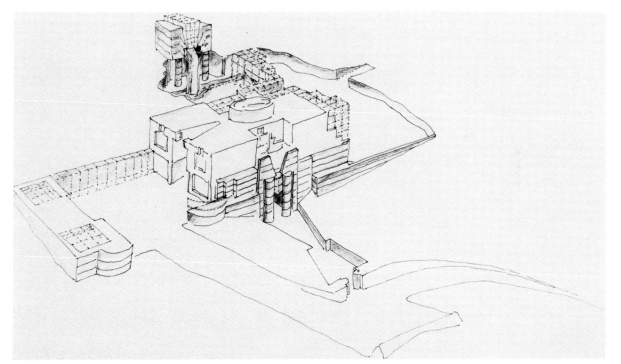

Figure 52. Michael Graves,
Plocek house, bird's-eye sketch.

The forms of the new work are elements culled not from our experience of the world (as were the cloud and the foliage) nor even from a kind of primordial experience of basic building (elements like support and entrance, prominent in others of Graves's early works); rather, these are forms lifted from architecture's own history. They are conventional forms: they were consciously designed by other people at other times to serve other architectural purposes. At first glance, then, Graves's new work would seem to be doing what I contend architecture must do, producing work in the present that constructs connections to work of the past. But by the peculiar way in which he makes the connection, Graves undercuts the kinds of connections I have been talking about.

In the Plocek house, Graves makes us unavoidably aware of the conventional architectural element of the keystone. The keystone shape appears in plan, sunk into the bank at the entrance and cut out of the block of the house itself. And a keystone that is "missing" from the screen wall at the entry "reappears" in the rear garden as the source for a waterfall. All of this forces upon us an awareness that the keystone is a made-up thing. We have all seen it before and just accepted it as a natural, fitting part of building. Now we have to admit to ourselves that the keystone is a conventional thing. We realize that it never had a necessary reason for being that way; we realize that it felt fitting to us only because we wanted it to feel so.

There is indeed a necessary, apart-from-our-preference reason for making keystones somewhat larger than the other stones of an arch, but that constructional reason is not the reason keystones feel right to us. They feel right for contingent reasons: the kinesthetic feeling that the arch pins the keystone the way our shoulders pin our neck and head when we lean on our outstretched palms; the feeling that the keystone provides a visual accent at an important point in the opening; the mere feeling of familiarity and expectedness—all of these reasons make a keystone feel right, but not one of them (or all of them together) is a sufficient reason why we must build in that way. As an analogy, recall the matter of murder in the law. There is a necessary, apart-from-our-preference reason why murder is wrong—its disrupting effect on society—but we punish murderers for other, contingent reasons in order that the punishment continue to make human sense to us. In like manner, there is a necessary reason for using an enlarged keystone, but we build that way for other, contingent reasons, so that each time a keystone is put into a building it will have been put there for a reason with human meaning. Graves's new work reminds us of how very contingent those reasons are.

As was true with the earlier work, this is a realization that can be liberating because it makes us aware that we are free to create virtually anything. But it also makes us aware of how really baseless it is to do so. For recall what conventional elements like key-stones (and legal principles and game rules) do: they provide us with a scrim that lets us go on believing in the worth of what we do. Graves's work, at every turn, shows us how evanescent, how arbitrary is that scrim. In sum, Graves's early work showed us how arbitrary is the process by which we impart meaning. His latest work shows us the arbitrary system we have constructed to scrim that arbitrariness from ourselves.

Let me push this critique one more step. Up to now I've dealt only with the six characteristics of an architecture of convention and not with its essential purpose, that of convincing us anew that architecture is worth doing. We've seen how, in order to be convinced anew, we need to be persuaded that a work of our time beats an older work at its own game. Do any of the postmodernist works persuade us that they are, in any sense, better than what the past produced?

Venturi has said repeatedly that because of economics and society's own values we are inevitably destined to build more cheaply and meanly than they did in the past. He says we ought to face that fact and make the most of it. Philip Johnson would probably deny that we have to build cheaply, but his new AT&T building, for all its expensive finishes, does not convince us that it outdoes the past. We look at the base of the tower, at all those Palladian motifs, and we can't escape the feeling that Palladio used them to better effect. With Eisenman's work, the possibility of making comparisons with older buildings does not even arise. And the work of Graves, for all its use of motifs from past architecture, deflects comparison because it uses those motifs for purposes that are so radically different. How can we say that a wedge-shaped entry court uses the convention of the keystone in a better way than do the arches of Michelangelo or Hawksmoor? Nor do the works of Hardy Holzman Pfeiffer engage their sources on a comparative basis. It would be meaningless to say that their work uses runway lights to better effect than airports. The two are not in any sense after the same thing.

But for me the most telling comparison comes in the work of Richard Meier (figure 53). Meier's houses, without intention, have all the characteristics of an architecture of convention. Their forms have that generalized address of slippage; the logic of their composition is not inexorable but has a certain contingency. To people aware of European modernist architecture Meier's houses vividly call to mind other buildings, in ways that are resonant. The forms leave open possibilities for speculation, even encourage us to do so. And in the smooth consistency of their vocabulary of forms, the houses present a scrim of conventions that is truly seamless. Meier's houses make us feel good about doing architecture.

But once one begins that comparative digging that I did with the Lawn and its

Figure 53. Richard Meier, house
near Old Westbury, Connecticut,
view. (Ezra Stoller, © ESTO)

predecessors, the feeling wells up that, even here, we haven't outdone the past. Any experience of a Meier house must bring to mind the white villas of Le Corbusier. Walking the ramps and rooms of the Villa Savoie, I felt the sheer suavity of that house, the way it moved my body through its spaces, the way its undulant or rigid walls felt around me, the knowing way its openings were placed and proportioned. And at first I felt that Meier's houses easily equaled this architecture, perhaps even went further in their address to the sheer pleasure of bodily movement and visual delight. But then, ineluctably, I had to recall Le Corbusier's intentions in building those white villas. I couldn't avoid the image of the *jardin suspendu* (figure 54), the outdoor space that was to bring light and health and vigor to the inhabitants of cramped cities. We smile at this image of the boxer working out under the eye of his companion. We know the naivete of that ideal, even its impossibility in the face of all that has happened since. But even as we smile, we must also realize how alive that ideal was to the people who held it, how much they were inspired by it, how much that is concrete and lasting they were able to achieve because they were motivated by it. For we realize that the ideal goes far beyond and before Le Corbusier. It was the dream of William Morris that workers could be as brothers. It has been the dream of generations of social democrats that government could be made the channel for society's best and most creative instincts. It was the dream of the Zionists and the Irish and the Russians and even of Jefferson himself that, once freed from the taint of a European past, people of good will could actually design a culture and nurture it into actuality. Seeing this we realize what a contradiction was the parallel modernist idea, the desire to be as a conduit for extrapersonal forces. But even with that, we are struck more by that faith in the efficacy of human volition, that faith that by the exercise of reason and good will we can decide how we want the world to be and that as humans we have the power to make it so.

Realizing this, we turn again to the Corbusier sketch, and our benign amusement is replaced by an almost anguishing poignancy. That sketch—and all the suavity and precision of the reality built from it—were in service to a deeply held aspiration, not just about how people could live but about how people could be. That sketch is a testament of faith in human possibility.

So then we turn back to the Meier house. The forms, for all their suavity and precision, are in service to no ideal about human possibility, and so we feel a gnawing absence. And it is an absence made more troubling by the realization that testimony to human potential is absent not just from this house but from most modern buildings and indeed from much of modern life.

Figure 54. Sketch by Le Corbusier
of a *jardin suspendu*.

The flawless precision of Meier's house forces us to admit that, for all the technological proficiency we have gained since the twenties, we have not been able to bend that skill to human purposes. We have not been able to make objects that will speak human values back to us. And so, encountering no new evidence that we can create things worth believing in, we have, by imperceptible stages, come close to deciding that it can't be done. We have come close to resigning ourselves to a material world that speaks only of forces beyond our control, of values that are not our own.

But to realize that this situation has been brought about by our own actions is to realize that it is within our power to rectify it. It *is* possible, even now, to produce architecture that gives testimony of human values. This book has tried to show one way in which that might be done. But whether these methods or some others are used, still the attempt must be made. We must find ways—in all areas of life—to engender in ourselves conviction about human values. We must find ways to convince ourselves anew of human possibility.

Notes

Chapter One

1. John Ruskin, *Elements of Drawing,* originally published in 1856. Page numbers are from an edition published by Scholarly Press (St. Clair Shores, Michigan) in 1972, which is a reprint of the 1893 edition by Maynard, Merrill (New York). A more accessible edition is that by Dover Publications (New York, 1971), which is a reprint from the Library Edition of *The Works of John Ruskin* (London: Smith, Elder, & Co., 1904).

2. Arthur Guptill, *Rendering in Pen and Ink* (New York: Watson-Guptill Publications, 1977). Page numbers and illustrations are taken from this new edition, which is a revision of the 1930 *Drawing in Pen and Ink* by the same publisher. That book is, in turn, derived from a 1928 edition of *Drawing in Pen and Ink* published by the Pencil Points Press, which was itself a compilation of a series of drawings done by Guptill during the twenties for *Pencil Points* magazine, the precursor of today's *Progressive Architecture.* All illustrations used here © 1976 by Watson-Guptill Publications.

3. Ruskin, *Elements,* p. 226.

4. Ibid.

5. Guptill, *Rendering,* pp. 26, 30.

6. Ibid., pp. 133ff.

7. Ruskin, *Elements,* p. 290.

8. Ibid., p. 305.

9. Ibid., p. 291.

10. Ibid., p. 305.

11. Guptill, *Rendering,* p. 83.

12. Ruskin, *Elements,* p. 301.

13. Guptill, *Rendering,* p. 158.

14. Not all architects use sketches in this way. Michael Graves, at a lecture in 1978, told of how suggestive he finds the practice

of sketching assemblages of architectural forms with no indication of their projective size—and how disconcerting it was to him once, while so sketching, to have a colleague reach over his shoulder and pencil in a stairway, thus establishing a scale for the drawing and limiting the possibilities that could be projected from it.

15. The attribution is by James F. O'Gorman in his *H. H. Richardson and His Office* (Cambridge, Mass.: The MIT Press, 1979; originally published, 1974).

16. David Varon, *Indication in Architectural Design* (New York: W. T. Comstock, 1916).

Chapter Two

1. Speech made by Heywood Hale Broun in Richmond, Virginia, March 1978. Reprinted from *Richmond Times-Dispatch*, 19 March 1978. Courtesy of Field Newspaper Syndicate.

Chapter Three

1. Foster Macy Johnson, *The Typographic Resources of a Country Printer* (Meriden, Conn.: Bayberry Hill Press, 1959). This is one of several books on typography that comment on (and sometimes lament) the ubiquity of Cheltenham in the years before and just after World War I, another being Alexander Lawson, *Printing Types: An Introduction* (Boston: Beacon Press, 1971).

2. J. L. Beigeleisen, *An Art Director's Workbook of Type Faces* (New York: ARCO Publications, 1976), p. 68.

3. Ibid.

Chapter Four

1. In fact, in this very area, the Uniform Commercial Code contains language that, in the states that have adopted it, supersedes all the reasoning of these cases in one stroke.

2. *LeLievre* v. *Gould* (1893) 1 Q.B. 497, quoted by Lord Buckmaster in *Donoghue* v. *Stevenson* (1932) A.C. 574—575. Here is a bit of coterie knowledge for the questing reader. These legal citations refer to various digests distributed by private publishers. "A.C." refers to the reports of the cases heard in the British Assizes Court; "Q.B.," the reports of the Queen's Bench; Maule & Selwyn covered certain courts in the nineteenth century, Meeson & Welsby covered certain other courts. In America, "N.E." stands for *North-East Reporter,* and so on. Thus 1 Q.B. 497 means page 497 of the first volume of Queen's Bench reports.

3. 5 Maule & Selwyn 198.

4. Interpretation by Lord Atkin in *Donoghue* v. *Stevenson* (1932) A.C. 587.

5. The phrase Levi uses in *An Introduction to Legal Reasoning.*

6. Lord Macmillan in *Donoghue* v. *Stevenson* (1932) A.C. 610.

7. Ibid., p. 609.

8. Or as Lord Atkin said in *Donoghue* v. *Stevenson,* "I venture to say that in the branch of the law which deals with civil wrongs, dependent in England at any rate entirely upon the application by judges of general principles also formulated by judges, it is of particular importance to guard against the danger of setting propositions of law in wider terms than is necessary, lest essential factors be omitted in the wider survey and the inherent adaptability of English law be unduly restricted. (1932) A.C. 583—584.

9. 2 Meeson & Welsby 519; 4 M. & W. 337.

10. *Longmeid* v. *Holliday,* 6 Ex. 765.

11. Lord Atkin's interpretation in *Donoghue* v. *Stevenson* (1932) A.C. 588.

12. 10 Meeson & Welsby 109.

13. Sir Frederick Pollock, *Law of Torts* (13th ed.), p. 570; as quoted by Lord Macmillan in *Donoghue* v. *Stevenson* (1932) A.C. 610.

14. 10 Meeson & Welsby 115.

15. Ibid., p. 116.

16. 6 Ex. 761.

17. Ibid., p. 764.

18. Ibid., p. 767–768.

19. Ibid., p. 768.

20. 6 N.Y. 397.

21. *Donoghue* v. *Stevenson* (1932) A.C. 598.

22. 5 L.R. Ex. 1.

23. Ibid., p. 5.

24. 11 L.R. Q.B. 503.

25. Ibid., p. 509.

26. Ibid., p. 508.

27. Ibid., p. 509.

28. Ibid., p. 513.

29. Ibid., p. 514.

30. Ibid., p. 512.

31. Ibid., p. 514.

32. Ibid., p. 516.

33. 106 L.T. 533.

34. Ibid., p. 539.

35. Ibid., p. 540.

36. Ibid., p. 541.

37. 221 Fed. 801.

38. Ibid.

39. 217 N.Y. 382; 111 N.E. 1050.

40. 111 N.E. 1053.

41. Ibid.

42. Ibid., p. 1052.

43. Ibid., p. 1053.

44. Ibid.

45. (1932) A.C. 562.

46. Ibid., p. 580.

47. 11 L.R. Q.B. 510.

48. (1932) A.C. 622.

49. Ibid.

Chapter Five

1. The terms and concepts are borrowed, with gratitude, from Harold Bloom, *The Anxiety of Influence* (New York: Oxford University Press, 1973).

2. I have culled these procedures from the presentations contained in two of the most venerated discussions of the law's workings: Benjamin Cardozo, *The Nature of the Judicial Process* (New Haven: Yale University Press, 1921), and Edward H. Levi, *An Introduction to Legal Reasoning* (Chicago: University of Chicago Press, 1949), with slight modifications taken from the comments of H. J. Berman and W. R. Greiner, *Nature and Functions of Law* (New York: Foundation Press, 1972); and Richard Dworkin, "The Model of Rules," *University of Chicago Law Review*, vol. 35 (1967).

Chapter Six

1. The same "big-little" analogy has also been pointed out by Vincent Scully in his *American Architecture and Urbanism* (New York: Praeger Publishers, 1969), p. 56; by Charles Moore; and by several professors and classmates of mine at Charlottesville, among others.

2. Frederick D. Nichols, *The Architectural Drawings of Thomas Jefferson* (Charlottesville: The University Press of Virginia, 1969).

3. Ibid.

4. All information on Marly comes from a French guidebook, *Marly*, by Jeanne and Alfred Marie, published in France in 1947 by Editions "Tel."

5. Comments by William Brubaker (". . . one big happy protesting family") in the design awards issue of *Progressive Architecture,* January 1970, p. 82.

6. "Another America," *Architectural Review,* July 1974, p. 28.

7. "On-campus Living: A Test of Multiple Choice," *Interiors,* November 1974, pp. 86—89.

8. Donlyn Lyndon, "Five Ways to People Places," *Architectural Record,* September 1975.

9. Kent C. Bloomer and Charles W. Moore, *Body, Memory, and Architecture* (New Haven: Yale University Press, 1977), p. 116.

10. The fountain has since been decked over with wooden boards, a layer of associations giving way to the practical requirement for more outdoor dining space. It is a pity that the renovation work was not done in a way that would suggest associations to replace those of the Mexican courtyard. As it now stands, the space has the ad hoc look of a problem "solved," but solved without a governing, overall conception.

Epilogue

1. William LaRiche, in his essay "Architecture as the World Again?" (in *Five Architects;* New York: Wittenborn & Co., 1972, p. 41), proposes that the beam, the bottom flange of which aligns with the top of a parallel hedge at the property line, "completes" that hedge. And the undulant soffit, by occurring in the gap in a line of trees, likewise completes that row—in addition to suggesting one of the favorite contours of the Cubist painters.

Bibliography

1. On Beaux-Arts and Scenographic Design

For an overview of drawing in general, see:

Rosenberg, Jakob. *On Quality in Art: Criteria of Excellence Past and Present*. Princeton: Princeton University Press, 1967.

Drawing handbooks from this specific period include:

Harding, J. D. *Elementary Art*. London, 1834. A very early handbook by one of Ruskin's drawing masters.

Holme, Charles, ed. *Sketches by Samuel Prout*. London: "The Studio," Ltd., 1915. Prout, a contemporary of Harding, pioneered a sketching style that proved to be highly influential.

Ruskin, John. *Elements of Drawing*. New York: Dover Publications, 1971 (reprint).

Guptill, Arthur. *Rendering in Pen and Ink*. Edited by Susan E. Meyer. New York: Watson-Guptill Publications, 1977 (revised edition).

Maginniss, Charles B. *Pen Drawing: An Illustrated Treatise*. Boston: Bates & Guild Co., 1903.

Magonigle, H. van Buren. *Architectural Rendering in Wash*. New York: Charles Scribner's Sons, 1921. Probably the best account of what was involved in executing the ink-and-wash drawings illustrated in the following book:

Drexler, Arthur, ed. *The Architecture of the Ecole des Beaux-Arts*. Cambridge, Mass.: The MIT Press, 1977. The drawings in this book provide a contrast to those shown in the following two books.

Goodhue, Bertram Grosvenor. *A Book of Architectural and Decorative Designs by Bertram Grosvenor Goodhue*. New York: Architectural Book Publishing Co., 1924.

O'Gorman, James F. *H. H. Richardson and His Office*. Cambridge, Mass.: The MIT Press, 1979 (originally published, 1974).

Handbooks on architectural design of the period include:

Batchelder, Ernest A. *The Principles of Design*. New York: The Macmillan Co., 1904.

Curtis, N. C. *Architectural Composition*. Cleveland: J. H. Jansen Co., 1908.

Edwards, A. Trystan. *Style and Composition in Architecture*. London: Alec Tiranti Ltd., 1952. One of a long series of books by Edwards.

Gaudet, Julien. *Elements et théorie de l'architecture*. Paris: Librairie de la construction moderne, 1929 (sixth edition). A compilation of the lectures of one of the greatest teachers at the Ecole des Beaux-Arts.

Harbeson, John F. *The Study of Architectural Design*. New York: Pencil Points Press, 1926. A book that both explains and advocates the Beaux-Arts teaching methods—and gives a glimpse of life in the *atelier*.

Mayeux, Henri. *La composition décorative*. Paris, 1904.

Pickering, Ernest. *Architectural Design*. New York: Wiley & sons, 1933.

Robertson, Howard. *The Principles of Architectural Composition*. New York: Chemical Publishing Co., 1924.

Robinson, John Beverly. *Principles of Architectural Composition*. New York: Chemical Publishing Co., 1899.

Van Pelt, John Vredenburgh. *A Discussion of Composition, Especially as Applied to Architecture*. New York: The Macmillan Co., 1902.

Varon, David. *Indication in Architectural Design*. New York: W. T. Comstock, 1916.

For an analysis of Beaux-Arts design, see:

Van Zanten, David. "Le système des Beaux-Arts." *L'architecture d'aujourd'hui,* November—December 1976.

_____. "Architectural Composition at the Ecole des Beaux-Arts from Charles Percier to Charles Garnier," in *The Architecture of the Ecole des Beaux-Arts,* ed. Arthur Drexler. Cambridge, Mass.: The MIT Press, 1977.

Other discussions of design methods include:

Scully, Vincent. *The Shingle Style and the Stick Style.* New Haven: Yale University Press, 1971 (revised edition). For a view of that particular period.

Collins, Peter. *Changing Ideals in Modern Architecture.* Montreal: McGill University Press, 1965. For a background and overview of the history of design approaches.

2. On Typography

Beigeleisen, J. L. *Art Director's Workbook of Type Faces.* New York: ARCO Publications, 1976.

Johnson, Foster Macy. *The Typographic Resources of a Country Printer.* Meriden, Conn.: Bayberry Hill Press, 1959.

Lawson, Alexander. *Printing Types: An Introduction.* Boston: Beacon Press, 1971. A good history of typefaces.

Zapf, Herman. *Manuale Typographicum.* Cambridge, Mass.: The MIT Press, 1970. Personal opinions and examples of work by the designer of the typeface used in this book.

3. On the Law

Berman, H. J., and Greiner, W. R. *Nature and Function of Law.* New York: Foundation Press, 1972. A basic modern textbook.

Cardozo, Benjamin. *The Nature of the Judicial Process.* New Haven: Yale University Press, 1921. An "orthodox" view of the law's workings, delivered in the rolling phrases of a great jurist, originally given as lectures at Yale.

Levi, Edward H. *An Introduction to Legal Reasoning.* Chicago: University of Chicago Press, 1949. A "revisionist" view of how the law works, by a former U.S. Attorney-General.

Dworkin, Richard. "The Model of Rules," *University of Chicago Law Review,* vol. 35 (1967). An example of the high level of commentary one finds in law journals.

Collins, Peter. *Architectural Judgement.* Montreal: McGill-Queens University Press, 1971. The book that broached the possibility that the law had something to teach architecture.

4. On Marly, the Lawn, and Kresge College

Marie, Jeanne and Alfred. *Marly.* Paris: Editions "Tel," 1947.

Nichols, Frederick D. *The Architectural Drawings of Thomas Jefferson.* Charlottesville: The University Press of Virginia, 1969.

Ware, Isaac. *The Four Books of Andrea Palladio's Architecture.* New York: Dover Publications, 1964. A reprint of the "London Palladio" of 1738.

Woodbridge, S. "How to Make a Place." *Progressive Architecture,* May 1974, pp. 76–83.

5. On Modernism in the Arts

Three of the most explicit statements of sixties modernism are these:

Fried, Michael. *Three American Painters.* Exhibition catalog, Fogg Museum, Harvard University, 1965.

_____. "Art and Objecthood," *Artforum,* no. 5 (summer 1967).

Greenberg, Clement. "Modernist Painting," in Battcock, Gregory, ed. *The New Art.* New York: E. P. Dutton, 1973.

Other views of modernism include:

Greenberg, Clement. *Art and Culture.* Boston: Beacon Press, 1961.

Krauss, Rosalind. *Terminal Iron Works: The Sculpture of David Smith.* Cambridge, Mass.: The MIT Press, 1971.

Steinberg, Leo. *Other Criteria: Confrontations with Twentieth Century Art.* New York: Oxford University Press, 1972.

6. On Postmodernism in Architecture

Probably the best overviews are contained in:

Scully, Vincent. *The Shingle Style Today.* New York: George Braziller, 1974.

Stern, Robert A. M. *New Directions in American Architecture.* New York: George Braziller, 1977 (revised edition).

For the views of individual architects, see:

Venturi, Robert. *Complexity and Contradiction in Architecture.* New York: Museum of Modern Art, 1966. The book that changed all the rules of architectural discourse, and made possible the kinds of discussion contained in this book.

_____, Denise Scott Brown, and Steven Izenour. *Learning from Las Vegas.* Cambridge, Mass.: The MIT Press, 1972.

Eisenman, Peter. *The Formal Basis of Modern Architecture.* Unpublished Ph.D. dissertation, Trinity College, Cambridge, England, 1963. This and the following entry are two of the most accessible entrees to the stimulating thoughts of Peter Eisenman—unfortunately, not widely available.

———. "Notes on a Conceptual Architecture II." Manuscript, 1972.

LaRiche, William. "Architecture as the World Again?" in *Five Architects.* New York: Wittenborn & Co., 1972. On the early work of Michael Graves.

Colquhoun, Alan. "From Bricolage to Myth: Or How to Put Humpty-Dumpty Together Again." *Oppositions 12* (spring 1978). On Graves's later work.

Eisenman, Peter. "The Graves of Modernism." *Oppositions 12* (spring 1978). A different view of Graves's later work.

7. Alternatives to Modernism—Sources of Ideas

Foucault, Michel. *The Order of Things.* New York: Vintage Books, 1973. Proposes that we can think in ways wholly unlike the ways we think now.

Lévi-Strauss, Claude. *The Raw and the Cooked.* New York: Harper & Row, 1969. My introduction to the idea that there are other ways to explain our actions than the way we explain them to ourselves.

Lakatos, Imre. "The History of Science and Its Rational Reconstruction." *Boston Studies in the Philosophy of Science,* vol. 8. Demonstrates that there are many ways of making sense of what we did in the past.

Bloom, Harold. *The Anxiety of Influence.* New York: Oxford University Press, 1973. An example of "reconstructing history."

Eliot, T. S. "Tradition and the Individual Talent." *Selected Essays, 1917–1932.* New York: Harcourt, Brace, 1932. A view surprisingly consonant with Bloom's on the extent to which history can be reread.

Sennett, Richard. *The Fall of Public Man.* New York: Alfred A. Knopf, 1977. Shows that people in the past were able to derive feelings of conviction from seeing a pattern of behavior enacted—even while being aware that such a pattern came into existence only because of their choice to act in that certain way.

Vidler, Anthony. "The Architecture of the Lodges: Ritual Form and Associational Life in the Late Enlightenment," *Oppositions 5* (summer 1976). An example of the conscious acting that Sennett describes.

Sontag, Susan. "Against Interpretation" and "On Style," in *Against Interpretation.* New York: Farrar, Straus & Giroux, 1966. This and the following entry deal with the notion that one of the ways of making sense of experience is through the stylizing of that experience in art—and the notion that that whole enterprise can work for us only when we *will* it into working for us.

_____. "The Aesthetics of Silence." *Styles of Radical Will.* New York: Farrar, Straus & Giroux, 1969.

8. Alternatives to Modernism and Postmodernism in Architecture

Scully, Vincent. *American Architecture and Urbanism.* New York: Praeger Publishers, 1969. A view of how architecture spoke to us before modernism.

Anderson, Stanford. "Architecture and Tradition," in *The History, Theory, and Criticism of Architecture,* ed. Marcus Whiffen. Cambridge, Mass.: The MIT Press, 1966. A vision of what architecture must do if it is to speak to us today.

_____. "Louis I. Kahn in the 1960s," *Boston Society of Architects Journal,* no. 1 (1967). An analysis of how Kahn's early work fulfilled that vision, how his later work did not.

"Old Lamps for New." *Architectural Review,* November 1975. The lamps are Ruskin's— a ringing castigation of modernism, a provocative call for an architecture reflective of human values.

Suggestive ways for making architecture do just that:

Lyndon, Donlyn. "Five Ways to People Places." *Architectural Record,* September 1975, pp. 89—94.

Moore, Charles W., Gerald Allen, and Donlyn Lyndon. *The Place of Houses.* New York: Holt, Rinehart & Winston, 1974.

Illustration Credits

34. Courtesy of Charles Moore.

35. Courtesy of William Turnbull.

36. Courtesy of William Turnbull.

37. Photo © by Morley Baer.

38. Courtesy of William Turnbull.

39. Drawing by John Kyrk, courtesy of Charles Moore.

40. Photo © by Morley Baer.

41. Photo © by Morley Baer.

42. Courtesy of William Turnbull.

43. Rollin R. LaFrance photo.

44. By permission of Venturi and Rauch.

45. Louis Checkman photo.

46. Norman McGrath photo.

47. Cervin Robinson photo.

48. Cervin Robinson photo.

49. David Morton photo.

50. Courtesy of Peter Eisenman.

51. Courtesy of Michael Graves.

52. Courtesy of Michael Graves.

53. Ezra Stoller, © ESTO.

54. With the kind permission of Architectural Publishers Artemis, Zurich.

Index